NO MORE HEROES

NO MORE HEROES

Madness & Psychiatry in War

RICHARD A. GABRIEL

HILL AND WANG · NEW YORK

A division of Farrar, Straus and Giroux

Library of Congress Cataloging-in-Publication Data
Gabriel, Richard A.
No more heroes.
Bibliography: p.
1. Psychiatry, Military. I. Title.
U22.3.G33   1987   616.85'212   86-33568

*To Kathie, my wife of twenty years,
who still remains a mystery while being the
most delightful discovery of all*

CONTENTS

You're dealing here with complicated psychological states. No man in battle is really sane. The mind-set of the soldier on the battlefield is a highly disturbed mind, and this is an epidemic of insanity which affects everybody there, and those not afflicted by it die very quickly.
—William Manchester,
Marine, World War II

Discipline keeps enemies face to face a little longer, but it cannot supplant the instinct of self-preservation and the sense of fear that goes with it. Fear! There are officers and soldiers who do not know it, but they are people of rare grit. The mass shudders because you cannot suppress the flesh. —Ardant Du Picq, 1872

The older I get, the sadder I feel about the uselessness of it all, but in particular the deaths of my comrades. . . . I thought I had managed all right, kept the awful things out of my mind. But now I'm an old man and they come out from where I hid them. Every night.
—A World War I veteran

NO MORE HEROES

Introduction

One of the most important measures of an army's combat effectiveness is how well its soldiers endure the storm of horror that washes over them in the sea of battle. To the individual soldier all war is small war comprised of hundreds of small-unit engagements in which the ability of individual soldiers to withstand the stress of battle is crucial to the unit's success or failure. In an age where military planners often emphasize the technology of war—the killing power of modern weaponry—it is all too often forgotten that the effectiveness of any weapon, no matter how destructive, is ultimately dependent upon the ability of a single soldier or small group of soldiers to make it work. And when soldiers manage for even a short time to withstand the stress of combat and make these weapons work, the destructive power of a modern conventional armed force surpasses anything which mankind has heretofore known in the long history of war. Technology, no matter how destructive or sophisticated, has yet to succeed in replacing the human element in achieving success on the field of battle.

The difficulty is that human beings are very fragile. History teaches that no matter how well trained the soldier is, no matter how cohesive his units, no matter how good and technically proficient his leaders are, men in battle will succumb to the stresses and strains inflicted upon them by their horribly destructive environment. Indeed, military history amply demonstrates that no one is immune to battle stress. Given enough time in combat, every soldier will eventually suffer a mental collapse.

The only question that today's military planners can realistically address is how to prevent the fearfully high rates of battle-shock breakdown from overwhelming an army's combat abilities. While strong, cohesive, disciplined, and well-led units can prevent rapid collapse and operate effectively for a while before suffering psychiatric casualties, the real challenge for military psychiatry is how to treat those who have broken under stress and quickly return them to battle. All other concerns are secondary.

In World War II, for example, American fighting forces lost 504,000 men from the fighting effort because of psychiatric collapse. That is a number sufficient to man fifty combat divisions! When measured against the stress and lethality of the modern battlefield, World War II battles pale in comparison. In the 1973 Arab-Israeli war, almost a third of Israeli casualties overall were due to psychiatric reasons. The same was true among the opposing Egyptian forces. In the 1982 incursion into Lebanon, Israeli psychiatric casualties were twice as high as the number of dead; psychiatric casualties accounted for 27 percent of the total wounded casualties. Projections for purely conventional-war scenarios involving Soviet and NATO forces in Central Europe suggest that the number of psychiatric casualties may reach between 40 and 50 percent of total casualties on both sides! In a scenario in which "limited" nuclear weapons are used in Central Europe, the number of psychiatric casualties can reasonably be expected to increase even further. The loss of men from psychiatric debilitation is fast reaching crisis proportions. As war becomes more destructive and the battlefield more lethal with each new generation of weapons, the number of men lost to the fighting effort as a result of mental collapse grows, threatening to reduce drastically the combat power of the fighting forces and, in some instances, to overwhelm it altogether. The problem of psychiatric breakdown in battle is thus becoming one of central importance for any military force that can reasonably expect to engage in battle in the future.

Given the importance of preventing and treating combat-stress casualties and the considerable experience armies have had with the problem since at least 1905, one might assume that armies would have worked out relatively successful strategies. All modern armies have plans, doctrines, and medical assets to deal with the problem. Yet military psychiatry is still a developing discipline in terms of definitively determining which mechanisms work best. While there is little doubt that concerned military planners in every army make some effort to study the experiences of other armies, the effort has been less than systematic or complete.

Moreover, the doctrines and practices of each army are, quite naturally, far more the result of its own battle experiences and the quality and direction of the broader field of psychiatry within its own country than of any systematic attempt to study and incorporate information available from military history or the experiences of other armies. That is why there exists no comprehensive written history of military psychiatry that addresses the development of combat psychiatry cross-culturally. That is also why there are no books that offer a comparative in-depth treatment of the subject against the background of historical experience.

This work begins with an attempt to convey an understanding of the human dimension of combat in modern war. The face of battle has changed so drastically since the end of World War II that unless one clearly understands its nature and the role of the human psyche in trying to deal with the stress imposed upon it by armed combat, no further progress is possible. If military planners are to be able to deal with the problem of military effectiveness, they must first understand the impact of modern war and the limitations that are imposed by the nature of this warfare and the very fragile nature of the human psyche. It is entirely possible that at some time very near in the future—if, indeed, we have not already reached it—we shall reach the point where war is truly obsolete, a point where warfare simply becomes impossible for the human being to endure and perform. It is already abundantly clear that warfare has its limits and chief among these is the ability of human beings to remain sane and functional amid the horror that battle necessarily entails.

Chapter 2 addresses the problem of psychiatric breakdown in battle from a historical perspective. There is a tendency of modern men to regard the problem of mental collapse under fire as pertaining only to recent generations of soldiers. In fact, a historical analysis of war reveals that men have always succumbed to the strain of battle and that armies have always suffered some form of diminished combat power because of it. What is particularly interesting is that the symptoms of psychiatric debilitation throughout history have remained remarkably constant. Soldiers not only have always collapsed in battle but have done so in precisely the same ways that they do today. If it were possible to transport a military psychiatrist back to the times of the Roman and Greek armies, there is little he would find in dealing with combat shock with which he was not already familiar.

Chapter 3 examines the nature of combat shock. There is a tendency on the part of both civilian and military leaders to remain unaware of the degree to which large numbers of soldiers are debilitated in battle by psychiatric collapse. There is also the widespread belief that mental collapse in war is, at worst, a temporary and transitory problem that is rapidly and easily cured. In fact, in every one of America's wars in this century the rates of psychiatric collapse among soldiers have exceeded the number killed in action. Moreover, the dynamics of psychiatric collapse reveal a condition that inflicts terrible suffering upon soldiers, suffering from which many never recover. Finally, future wars will most likely incapacitate more soldiers through shock than through killing and wounding.

Chapter 4 addresses the way armies have traditionally dealt with the problem of battle shock. The analysis begins prior to the Civil War and moves to a consideration of how armies intend to deal with the problem in the future. The unfortunate conclusion of the analysis is that military psychiatry in war has simply not been very successful in working out solutions to a growing problem.

Chapter 5 looks at the future of military psychiatry and considers whether any program to prevent and treat battle shock has any realistic chance of succeeding amid the lethality generated on the battlefield by modern weaponry. There is no doubt that past approaches to the problem will no longer work except under conditions of low-intensity conflict. Just where that leaves the individual soldier of the future, to say nothing of the best-laid plans of military planners, is a question whose implications stagger the imagination. Perhaps most horrifying of all, the main directions of military psychiatry are pointing to a chemical solution to the problem, the development of drugs that will prevent the onset of battle-shock symptoms and, in the process, completely change man's psychic constitution. The specter of a chemically changed soldier whose mind has been made over in the image of a true sociopathic personality cannot be realistically ignored.

In analyzing the experiences of armies throughout history, one cannot but be struck by the persistence of combat-stress reactions almost regardless of what military psychiatrists attempt to do about them. Nor is one less amazed by the inventiveness of the human psyche in seeking to save itself from battlefield danger by generating all kinds of symptoms and behavior which get the soldier removed from the very horror that generated the conditions in the first place. Moreover, there seems to be a clear connection between those symptoms which the soldier and psychiatric diagnosticians on the battlefield recognize as "legitimate" reasons for removing the soldier from battle and the precise symptoms which soldiers manifest when subjected to the stress of battle. And there is simply no reason to believe that the inventiveness of the human psyche in this area has been exhausted. New conditions of stress will almost certainly generate new symptoms along with the classic symptoms which have emerged throughout military history. The circle is as complete as it is vicious.

All this raises the question whether military psychiatrists may simply be wasting their time. It seems clear that if one takes the view that defining and recognizing certain symptoms as reasons to remove the soldier from combat will simply result in generating these symptoms—which, in turn, means that psychiatric cases will occur and almost always overburden the medical services—why not, one might suggest, simply enforce a harsh set of diagnostic criteria, as the Soviet Army does and the German Army did, and force the soldier to return to the fighting at gunpoint if necessary? After all, that is precisely what the Soviet and American armies intend to do with soldiers who have received a fatal dose of radiation from nuclear weapons. To be sure, these soldiers will eventually die—perhaps within a matter of four to five days. So why not get a few more days of fighting out of them?

The argument against using harsh diagnostic criteria is that cumulative stress will eventually manifest itself in some way regardless of what is done. Thus, if one does not treat acute anxiety it will manifest itself sooner or later in such things as self-inflicted wounds, higher numbers of accidental injuries, frostbite, incapacitating headaches, AWOL, and even venereal disease. Granted that such expectations are correct, it is still unclear that the time required for such manifestations to occur would not be longer than the time lost by treating the psychiatric casualty in the first place.

Moreover, it may be easier to treat the physical debilitation—frostbite, venereal disease, etc.—than to treat the psychiatric conditions which military psychiatry currently addresses. Finally, treating physical conditions may succeed more rapidly than treating the underlying psychiatric disturbance that provoked their manifestation. It is true as well that with physical injuries the soldier obtains much of the same treatment—rest, food, sleep, a respite from battle—that he would receive as a purely psychiatric casualty. In short, stringent diagnostic criteria will not eliminate psychiatric casualties but might make their treatment easier while at the same time permitting the psychiatrically broken soldier to function for longer periods of time in the battle zone. The price, of course, is a diminished sense of sensitivity to human suffering that allows for men to be driven remorselessly to their deaths when they could have been saved.

While it is unlikely that this debate will be resolved easily—indeed, the debate along these lines has hardly begun in earnest—what partial evidence there is from military history suggests that there may very well be something to be gained from pursuing it. In World War I, for example, almost all major combatants used a very harsh diagnostic definition of what constituted a legitimate psychiatric casualty. In general, a soldier manifesting psychiatric symptoms had to be found to be suffering from some organic damage before he was granted relief from duty. Thus the attribution of psychiatric debilitation to such things as shell shock, microbleeding in the brain, and contusions to the brain. What is interesting is that most armies in World War I suffered about the same level of manpower loss for psychiatric reasons, between six to nine men per thousand casualties, a comparatively low rate by today's standards.

By World War II, the U.S. Army and some others had changed their diagnostic definitions to ones that were far more lenient, in that they moved beyond purely physical causes for mental ailments to include emotional and psychogenic causes. Other former World War I combatants, such as Germany and the U.S.S.R., retained their harsh definitions. Comparing the performance of these two sets of combatants in World War II is very illuminating.

In World War I, the American Army, relying on the harsh diagnostic categories of other armies, suffered a psychiatric casualty rate of about nine men per thousand. In World War II, after the U.S. Army had adopted a more general and lenient diagnostic system, it suffered a psychiatric casualty rate of thirty-six men per thousand, a rate four times higher. The Germans and Russians in World War I suffered about the same rate of psychiatric casualties as other armies, about nine per thousand. Yet, during World War II, both of these armies retained their harsh diagnostic definitions of psychiatric breakdown. Interestingly, in World War II the Soviet and German armies had about the same rate of psychiatric casualties as they did in World War I, about nine per thousand. By any standard, the manpower loss to psychiatric collapse was simply much lower in armies that had retained harsh diagnostic definitions. If the German and Soviet armies suffered large numbers of collateral psychiatric casualties—soldiers whose psychiatric symptoms manifested themselves in more direct physical symptoms, such as accidents, disease, frostbite, etc.—such collateral casualties were not sufficient to weaken their battle performance.

None of this is to suggest that armies can dispense with military psychiatry. What it does suggest is that in an era of high-intensity warfare of greatly increased lethality some thought must be given to redefining the role of military psychiatry in the battle zone to accommodate very harsh realities. The sad truth is that soldiers have to some extent always been dispensable in war. Certainly, loss rates are somewhat predictable for certain kinds of operations. Perhaps we have simply reached a point where the reality is that soldiers who suffer psychiatric difficulties are more dispensable than others, a cruel proposition at best. Especially so in light of the evidence which suggests that there are no significant personality traits which immunize the soldier to psychiatric breakdown. All men are at risk of mental collapse when placed in the environment of modern war.

In the end, of course, there is no answer; there are only victims. The cruel realities of past wars have grown exponentially more cruel as nations face the future. The human material of warfare has not changed; nor is it likely to. The men who stood at Meggido or Cannae or Waterloo were no different from those who will be asked to stand on future battlefields. They will have the same hopes and the same fears and all too many will suffer the same fate. What has changed, of course, is the nature, tempo, and lethality of war. In the past, weaponry was fashioned to the human capacity to use it. Now, the human capacity must be refashioned to utilize the weaponry. This has led the military establishments of the world to begin searching for a chemical solution to the problem, a drug that will make it possible to banish fear in the soldier by controlling his brain chemistry. If these efforts succeed, man will be poised on the edge of a new and threatening frontier, one that, if crossed, will forever change man's nature and cost him his soul. If the efforts are allowed to proceed, we will remake man in our own image and the consequences will be horrifying. And we will create a whirlwind of military violence, destruction, and human suffering such as the world has never seen.

1

The Face of Modern War

Americans are a fortunate people, especially when it comes to war. Our collective psyche has been only lightly touched by war. In all its major wars the United States has lost relatively small numbers of men killed and wounded in comparison with other nations, to say nothing of being able to avoid the death and suffering of civilians and the mass destruction of property that invariably accompanies a war fought in one's own country. Except for the Civil War, in those few instances where we have gone to war we have fought on foreign soil. A consequence of this fortunate historical experience is that we are largely unaware of the human costs of war, counted in blood, mangled bodies, and the minds of soldiers driven insane by terror.

The disparity of experience with war between the United States and other nations is great indeed. In the six-week battle for the city of Berlin in 1945, the Soviet Army lost more casualties than America lost in all its foreign wars combined. The Israelis, in eighteen days of combat in the 1973 Yom Kippur war, had twice as many casualties in proportion to their population as the United States did in ten years of war in Vietnam. The Iran-Iraq war has claimed more dead in five years than all the dead lost by the United States in World War II, Korea, and Vietnam combined. More men were lost in six hours in the first Battle of the Somme in 1916 by British forces than were lost to hostile fire in Vietnam. We have been a very fortunate people indeed.

This lack of a genuine bloody experience with war has produced in the American psyche a dangerously naïve view of combat and its human costs. It is a naïveté nurtured by a powerful communications establishment—television and movies—which increasingly serves as the single informational anchor in the lives of the most geographically mobile people on earth. The images seen on television comprise more and more of the informational ken of the American people. What few sources of counterinformation are available are increasingly ignored or overwhelmed by the sheer number of hours most Americans spend in front of the television set or at the movies. More and more of what is seen on the electronic screen is accepted as reality. The electronic village is here.

The result is an unfortunate and colossal ignorance of the true horror of battle coupled with a historical faith in technology, especially military weaponry, which works to make war seem remote, bloodless, impersonal, and highly technical. Watching scenes of American carrier aircraft shooting Libyan ships out of the water at ranges in excess of forty miles with highly sophisticated electronic missiles, Americans can, perhaps, be forgiven their ignorance. Television and movies provide a view of war that has become the only experience of war for the majority of Americans.

While only the truly insane would regard a nuclear war as tolerable, most Americans share the belief that a conventional war is acceptable. The view that conventional war is a fitting military response to provocation is rooted in our limited experience of even conventional conflicts. After all, World Wars I and II, Korea, and Vietnam were, at least for us, quite tolerable in terms of the human costs simply because those costs were so much lower than those of any other military participant. Further, our conventional wars were wars in which the individual soldier seemed able to control his own destiny; wars in which training and native wit could outfox the firepower and military professionalism of our adversaries; wars in which the citizen soldier was largely able to cope; wars in which heroism and courage were still believed possible and counted for something.

But the realities of today's wars are vastly different. Modern conventional weapons developed since the end of World War II are so lethal and destructive that, in the words of a U.S. Army manual, "conventional war has unconventional effects." As the famous British military analyst John Keegan has noted, there are any number of conventional weapons in use today whose destructive power is equal to or greater than that of nuclear weapons. The F-4 Phantom fighter plane, for example, can deliver destructive power greater than that afforded by a low-yield nuclear cruise missile.[1] Modern artillery, when fired in mass, is more destructive than nuclear artillery rounds, and even the destructive power of the neutron bomb can be readily exceeded by a squadron of aircraft dropping conventional Fuel Air Munitions. The conventional chemical warfare capabilities of any number of military establishments, including those of the underdeveloped nations, can exterminate civilian and military populations much larger than those of Hiroshima or Dresden in only slightly more time than it took to destroy them with bombs. The horrible fact is that conventional war today is as far removed in its intensity, scope, and lethality from World War II as World War II was removed from the Battle of Waterloo.

Most Americans remain ignorant of the realities of modern conventional war and paradoxically see it as a real alternative to nuclear war. Equally troubling is their genuine national fascination with machines and technology of all kinds, especially the technology of war. In no other country is the belief more deeply seated that victory belongs to the side with the best and most sophisticated military gadgetry. Our romance with machines, rooted strongly in our own industrial and military history, has led us to fail to appreciate the human dimension and costs of war. It has also led us to ignore the question whether normally sane men can retain their sanity while engaged in battle. This is a question of singular relevance in view of the fact that in every war since World War I more American soldiers have become psychiatric casualties than were killed by enemy shells and bullets. Never having experienced the terror of battle to any great degree, we have never as a people truly gazed into the face of modern war as other countries have.

Goodbye, World War II

World War II was the last time Americans had any serious experience with war. It seems logical to examine today's military capabilities in relation to those of that war. Some may believe that the wars in Korea and Vietnam were equally terrible. Perhaps. But as we shall see later, by any standard of military action they were not. Even the losses were marginal by historical standards. It is sobering to remember in this regard that during the Korean War two and a half times as many Americans were killed by gunshot wounds within the United States as on the battlefield. During the Vietnam War the figure was six times as many. Indeed, there was considerable truth to the joke among Vietnam soldiers that one was safer in Saigon than in New York! Whatever else the wars in Korea and Vietnam were, they were not serious wars. Indeed, we lost both of them with no apparent damage to the international power of the country. If World War II is used as the standard, it becomes possible to measure just how far we have come in the development of battlefield weapons for the future. The distance is alarmingly great.

There is an old military adage that when it comes to

combat, "quantity has a quality all its own." In a major conventional war in Central Europe, the numbers of men and equipment that would be involved suggests that conventional war has changed qualitatively over the years.[2] If it is assumed that one side or the other gains some degree of surprise, thus reducing mobilization time to a minimum, on the first day of battle 1.7 million men on both sides would engage each other in combat. After two days, when the ready reserves of the major combatants would have been committed, the number of men involved in the fighting would grow to 2.8 million. If the fighting lasted ten full days, the number of combatants would jump to almost 6 million. In thirty days, after both sides had ample time to commit their substantial reserves, the number of men trying desperately to kill one another would increase to more than 15 million soldiers at one time. History has never recorded so many men locked in combat in so short a time. Given that both sides understand that once war breaks out the side that puts the most men in the field will have a decided advantage, it is difficult to see how the quantitative escalation in manpower can be stopped once it begins.

Modern armies have more machines of destruction at their disposal than any other armies in history. There are, for example, 13,500 main battle tanks in the NATO inventory compared to 42,600 for the Warsaw Pact countries; 560 NATO attack helicopters to 960 for the Warsaw Pact; 32,000 antitank guided missile launchers for the Warsaw Pact compared to 12,300 for the NATO forces; 33,000 NATO armed armored personnel carriers to 75,000 for the Warsaw Pact; 35,000 Warsaw Pact artillery pieces to 11,000 for the NATO forces; and 6,550 high-performance strike aircraft on the side of the Warsaw Pact compared to 3,100 similar aircraft in NATO. Whatever else conventional war in Central Europe would bring, it would result in the largest concentration of war machines ever committed to a single battle.

On the first day of fighting, both sides will be able to engage almost 20,000 modern main battle tanks, and after thirty days, the number of tanks on both sides would increase to 56,000. Attempting to counter these armored battle cruisers will be antitank missile crews who will be able to fire 530,000 antitank guided missiles at one another. In the skies fighter aircraft will be as numerous as gnats. On the opening day of battle, each side could commit more than 4,000 strike aircraft, a figure which would double in less than a week as air reserves are committed.

All this manpower and machinery would be used within a battle zone less than seven hundred miles long and forty miles deep. Modern armies calculate that they need about 1,400 soldiers per mile of battlefront, actually fewer than the 1,700 maximum of World War II. However, it must be kept in mind that in a modern conventional war a greater percentage of a unit's manpower will actually be engaged in the killing than ever before. Moreover, the ability of today's soldier to deliver and sustain firepower has grown exponentially since 1945. For example, a Soviet motorized rifle division can deliver ten times the firepower at three times the rate of a similar World War II division. The same is true of NATO divisions. Compared to World War II, more men will be putting out far more firepower for longer periods over much greater distances and producing greater lethality.

This concentration of sheer military power is frightening enough, but it must be remembered that modern war is a war of speed, mobility, penetration, encirclement, and envelopment. The initial clash of armies will be followed within a few days by a flexing of the front line in which one side or the other will have to give way. Once units begin to give ground, they will be pressed back against units deployed in the rear. In a phenomenon not unlike that of ancient Greek phalanxes crashing together, the battlefield will begin to shrink as the size of the battle zone becomes compressed. When this happens, the number of targets in the battle zone will increase, creating a "target-rich environment," and the intensity of the battle will become even more ferocious.

It is equally important to realize that a large-scale modern conventional war will be fought in a radically different manner. World War II was a linear war in which combat occurred along a generally well-defined front line with usually safe rear areas. In the past, areas twenty miles behind the line were almost totally secure as long as the balance of airpower remained relatively intact. The enemy was clearly to the front at all times. Moreover, World War II was a tactical war in which most of the fighting was done by units of division size or less (approximately 10,000 men). The conventional war of the future presents a far different set of circumstances.

In modern conventional war, linear tactics will be replaced by "swirling tactics." The combat reach of modern armies is so long and the mobility of combat vehicles so great that armies must now plan to fight three battles at once. Both U.S. and Soviet combat doctrine requires that units be able to fight the "direct" battle—that is, to engage units directly to their front. But it also requires that they be able simultaneously to fight the "deep" battle, to reach out and strike deeply behind the enemy's lines with large combat forces in order to disrupt his timetables, supplies, and reinforcements. Of course, one side's deep battle is the other side's "rear" battle. Each army will have to deal with sizable enemy forces engaged in attacking its rear. Such forces will be inserted into rear areas by paradrop or helicopter or will break through the front lines and head for specific targets in the rear areas. Some idea of the ferocity of these "rear" battles can be gained from the fact that the units attacking the enemy's rear will be of division size or larger. Simultaneously, modern attack aircraft and helicopters will roam hundreds of miles behind enemy lines wreaking havoc with their large-caliber multi-barreled guns and guided rockets.

Accordingly, the entire battlefield will be highly unstable. It will be a war, not of fixed lines, but of swirling combat in which units will be expected to fight isolated from parent units. Units will be trapped, decimated, bypassed, isolated, and often expected to stand and fight until they can no longer do so. In short, it will not be a war of offense and defense as in World War II. It will be a war of meeting engagements in which all units will be expected to carry on a continuous offensive.

Modern conventional war will not be a tactical war in which most of the fighting is done by relatively small units of division size or less. Instead, it will be an operational-level war in which the scope of command and control will move back from the line divisions to the corps and theater commands. Corps will engage and fight battles as brigades did in World War II. Larger units will be committed at once for objectives of greater scope. More resources will be thrown at any one time into any given engagement. The shift from the tactical to the operational level of war will mean far more intense and destructive battles raging for longer periods of time over greater areas.

Under these conditions the zone of destruction—the area in which soldiers will be involved in combat and have a good chance of being killed or wounded—will increase. During World War I the zone of destruction extended five miles from the front at the maximum. By World War II it had increased to ten miles. In modern conventional war, the zone of destruction will extend to the depth of the entire front, about forty miles, and even beyond. During World War II, for example, a division commander had to worry about the forces deployed about ten to fifteen miles to his front. Today, he is responsible for locating and killing forces forty miles to his front and his "area of tactical interest" extends to almost sixty miles. Moreover, he has at his command weapons systems that can reach sixty miles to his front to engage and destroy enemy forces. Of course, so does his opponent.

Yet another element which distinguishes modern conventional war from World War II is the amount of fighting that will occur at night. In World War II, the soldier's ability to fight at night was severely limited by his ability to see. Mechanical means for locating the enemy were almost nonexistent except for primitive radars which could locate large formations of aircraft. The World War II soldier generally had no better means of fighting at night than did the soldiers of ancient Rome. As a consequence, most military action, as it had for centuries before, came to a halt at nightfall. To be sure, there were nighttime probes and reconnaissance patrols, but what little fighting there was was confined to very small units, and the darkness itself reduced the effectiveness of weaponry. All that has changed.

Today military forces are equipped with a wide range of electronic, laser, infrared, and optical devices that can turn the nighttime battlefield into day. Modern tank sights can easily locate a target in complete darkness at 3,500 yards, and the target is seen as easily as during daylight. Even when the target cannot be seen with optical enhancing devices, its silhouette can be discerned by infrared and laser sights. Modern weaponry, especially antitank missiles, can home in with deadly accuracy on the heat emitted by a vehicle's engine. One optical device, the Starlight scope, the size of a small telescope, can even discern the difference between a male and a female at over a thousand yards by the distinct differences in the heat given off by the pelvic areas of the two sexes. Furthermore, such night sighting devices are not confined to the heavy machines of war like the armored personnel carrier or the tank. In addition, every infantryman will be equipped with night-vision goggles.

The increased ability of military forces to see at night makes it possible, indeed mandatory, for large combat units to conduct military operations around the clock. Once engaged it will be increasingly difficult for units of any size to disengage, as the attacking forces will be able to continually locate them. The normal respite that soldiers throughout history had come to expect with the fall of night will come no more. War will be fought with almost the same intensity around the clock.

If the size, scope, and intensity of future conventional war has grown enormously, the reason, of course, is the weapons that are at the command of all truly modern armies. There are now weapons in the arsenal of the ordinary combat division that would turn even the most hardened of World War II commanders green with envy.

It is important to understand that the destructiveness of modern war and the tremendous stress it places upon the mind of the soldier do not depend upon having a war in which millions of men and machines are brought into battle. Indeed, the most likely types of conventional wars of the future will be small "brushfire wars" in which comparatively small numbers of combatants participate. However, the stress on the soldier will be the same, since the relative intensity of a division-size battle will be the same as in a corps-size battle. The changes in the nature of warfare have made almost any conventional war among modern military forces horribly intense. The weapons have become more destructive and out of proportion to the ability of the soldier to withstand them.

Artillery

Historically, artillery has always inflicted the most casualties on fighting troops. Almost 60 percent of total casualties in warfare since the invention of gunpowder have been caused by artillery. In World War II, more than half of all combat casualties were caused by this fighting arm. And the capacity of artillery to destroy has grown frighteningly since 1945. The artillery firepower of a maneuver battalion has doubled in lethality since World War II and the "casualty effect" has increased by 400 percent! The range of artillery guns, on average, has increased by 60 percent since 1945 and the "lethality coverage area," the zone in which death can be expected to occur, has increased by 350 percent.

The explosive power of artillery rounds has increased almost seven times. In World War II most artillery rounds had thicker casings and delivered some variant of TNT. Today, with the revolution in chemical and plastic explosives, the casings are thinner, so that a shell of the same caliber can deliver many times the explosive power on the target. A single round fired by the M-110A2 self-propelled artillery cannon is approximately equal in explosive power to that of the MK-81 250-pound bomb. On impact, a single artillery round will produce a crater twenty-five feet in diameter and ten feet deep, displacing over five thousand cubic feet of earth. Such a round can penetrate up to three feet of concrete or five inches of steel and send shrapnel out to a radius of three hundred feet. Almost all soldiers within a two-hundred-foot radius of an exploding round would be killed by shrapnel or concussion. Newer artillery munitions, such as the Beehive round, are lethal at even greater distances. Developed during Vietnam to deal with mass enemy attacks, the Beehive round is filled with 5,000 fléchettes, slender nail-like steel needles three inches long capable of pinning their targets to trees! If the Beehive round is set off above the heads of advancing troops, its lethality is even greater.

Modern artillery pieces are lighter, stronger, and far more mobile than they were in World War II, resulting in a revolution in mobile firepower. Today, a combat unit can take its artillery along with it as it advances. Moreover, an artillery unit can set up, bring its guns to bear, fire on a target, and move on in minutes to a new location, making it much more difficult for the enemy to destroy it by counterfire or air attack. Further, the rates of fire per gun have increased greatly, as the gun tubes are now made of stronger metal alloys. Projected rates of fire for modern artillery pieces approach five hundred rounds per day over a four-hour period, almost three times the World War II rate. The guns last longer, retain their sighting on target better, and don't overheat as badly. Less maintenance means more combat effectiveness.

The magnitude of artillery fire which modern armies can bring to bear staggers the imagination. If all artillery guns—from 81mm mortars to tank guns—are counted, the average combat division can mount almost five hundred guns firing at once. In World War I the number of guns per thousand men in a division was six; during World War II it climbed to about twelve. Today the number of guns per thousand men in a division exceeds thirty. To put this firepower in perspective, the Soviet Army is equipped to mass three hundred artillery pieces per single mile of combat frontage! The magnitude of artillery fire is further increased by the use of different types of fuses which increase its effectiveness. Thus, the variable-time or VT fuse can be used to cause shells to burst over the heads of troops, greatly magnifying their killing capacity. Proximity fuses allow a shell to sense when it is near its target and explode close to it, causing great damage without having to hit the target directly. Artillerymen can implant submunitions with delay fuses which will explode on either a random or a timed basis, thus denying large areas of the battlefield to the enemy.

The range of artillery projectiles has increased enormously. Both the M-107 and the M-110 are capable of hurling 175mm shells and 203mm shells twenty-three miles and twenty-two miles, respectively. With rocket-assisted shells, these ranges exceed twenty-five miles. These self-propelled artillery pieces can move under their own power at speeds of thirty-five miles an hour with a range of two hundred and twenty miles. The ability of mobile artillery to keep a retreating enemy easily within range far exceeds World War II capabilities.

Artillery shells are also far more accurate, and thus far more deadly, than in World War II. This has been made possible by linking sophisticated electronic sensors with computers. Hardly any artillery is fired by manual calculations anymore. Information is fed into the guns from electronic sensors, sometimes dropped miles away by aircraft, and computers instantly do multiple range and deviation calculations. Rounds rarely miss their targets anymore. The rapidity of fire has increased as well. In World War II it would take an average gun crew about six minutes to zero in on its target. Today an artillery battery can perform the same task in less than fifteen seconds, greatly reducing the chances that even a moving target will escape destruction. At the same time, of course, the means for delivering counterbattery fire on enemy artillery pieces have improved greatly. During World War II counterbattery fire was, at best, an uncertain thing. All artillery could do was fire in the direction of the roar or muzzle flashes of enemy guns and hope to saturate the area around the target sufficiently to knock out the gun. Today electronic devices can compute the position of artillery fire almost instantly and command guns to return fire on the battery. The days when artillery was placed safely behind the lines are over.

While there have been great improvements in the accuracy of artillery weapons, the unguided artillery round used to saturate specific areas has truly come into its own. The Russians first introduced the idea of mass rocket artillery fired in salvo. Their Katusha rocket launchers in World War II were ideal weapons for saturating large areas of the front while at the same time generating high rates of psychiatric casualties. Salvos of artillery rockets are highly effective for achieving surprise, delivering chemical weapons and counterbattery fire. Today a single Soviet battalion of eighteen BM-21 rocket launchers can fire 720 rounds almost seventeen miles in thirty seconds. Such a volley will put thirty-five tons of rockets on target and devastate an area 2,000 yards by 500 yards. Not to be outdone, the Americans have developed the Multiple Launch Rocket System (MLRS). With this system a single three-man crew can launch twelve rockets in less than thirty seconds. After each rocket is launched in ripple fire, the on-board computer will recalculate the trajectory for the next rocket. A salvo of twelve rockets contains 8,000 M-77 antipersonnel weapons which can be dispersed in midair above the target and saturate an area the size of six football fields in less than a minute. In another configuration, each rocket can dispense twenty-eight antitank mines. A third configuration allows each rocket to release almost ten SADARMs (Search And Destroy Armor Mines). Each of these SADARMs is a homing warhead which can locate a tank, guide itself to the target, and destroy it. By the time the MLRS rockets have hit their targets, the crew has driven the launcher to a new position where it can reload and fire again.

The destructive power of artillery cannot be underestimated. Today a division artillery complement can fire concentrations of artillery at three levels of intensity. If it fires at its lowest level (harassment), it is expected that 10 percent of the soldiers in the target area will be killed. At the second level of intensity (neutralization), it can kill 30 percent of the soldiers in the area of impact. If it fires at its most intense (destruction), the killing rate rises to 60 percent.

Among the most bizarre, yet effective, artillery munitions is the Copperhead artillery round, which can be fired from the M-109 155mm artillery piece. Once fired, it follows its normal ballistic trajectory until it begins to descend in the general area of the target. At this point the round will home in on its target by laser illumination. The Copperhead has the ability to hit a moving tank nineteen miles away. In tests, the round actually found its way into the open hatch of a moving tank!

Lastly, artillery serves in air defense. During World War II division air defense artillery could expect to control the airspace above its position for about a mile in any direction. Today it can control thirty-six times that space. In 1945 a typical American division carried sixty-four air defense weapons. Today a division has one hundred and thirteen, and Soviet divisions mount about 10 percent more. Almost all modern air defense guns have automatic guidance systems, radar, and optical sights. Some radar-controlled guns can fire sixty rounds in a single one-second burst. The M-163 Vulcan air defense gun, mounted on a self-propelled chassis, is a six-barreled 20mm cannon capable of firing 3,000 rounds a minute. It is equipped with an automatic telescope, a gyro-leading computing gunsight, and search radar. The radar has a range search time of one second and can detect a target at almost two miles with 100 percent accuracy!

Advances in technology since World War II have been so great that there is no comparison between artillery of that era and that found on the modern battlefield. As in the past, artillery can be expected to cause the lion's share of battlefield casualties. It will surely generate the largest number of psychiatric casualties as rates and accuracy of firepower increase. The Russians, who suffered terribly from enemy artillery in the two world wars, are even greater proponents of artillery than are armies of the West. While Americans refer to artillery as "the king of battle," the Russians, who have been its greatest victims all the way back to Napoleonic times, have dubbed it "the hammer of god." It has revolutionized the battlefield.

Tanks and Armored Fighting Vehicles

Of great importance on the modern battlefield is the presence of large numbers of tanks and other armored vehicles which complement the role of artillery in killing as many soldiers as possible. Modern tanks offer an unprecedented combination of firepower, shock action, and mobility. They can be expected to kill and be killed in numbers heretofore unknown.

The modern U.S. battle tank is about one-third heavier than its World War II counterpart, but its engines are twice as powerful. Accordingly, its horsepower-to-weight ratio is less and its ground pressure is also less. This means that its range and speed are much greater than that of World War II tanks. Today's tank can cruise at speeds approaching forty miles an hour for more than three hundred miles, a range three times that of World War II tanks. With the development of stabilized turrets and highly sophisticated gunsights, the modern tank can shoot on the run with a greater probability of hitting its target than a World War II tank firing from a standing position. The accuracy of bigger guns has also improved tremendously. In World War II a tank firing at a target fifteen hundred yards away had to fire thirteen rounds to achieve a 50 percent probability of hitting its target. Today, a modern tank will hit its target at that range with a single shot 98 percent of the time. Moreover, a World War II tank gun could penetrate only 4.8 inches of armor plate at fifteen hundred yards. Today a tank gun can easily penetrate 9.5 inches of armor plate at six thousand yards.

The size of tank guns has increased by at least one-third and the muzzle velocity of tank rounds has doubled. The use of laser range finders has increased the range of target sighting by over thirty times. For example, the Hughes thermogunsight mounted on the M-1 tank is capable of finding targets at two thousand yards, producing a clear target image in complete darkness or through smoke, fog, or rain. The probabilities of hitting a target have increased tenfold since World War II.

The improvement in the killing power of tank gun ammunition is amazing. New propellants and explosive compounds have made tank rounds many times more destructive than those available in World War II. Moreover, improvements in the understanding of ballistics has led to new types of tank ammunition undreamed of in 1945. The APDS (Armor Piercing Discarding Sabot) is one such round. Weighing forty-one pounds, it leaves the gun muzzle at 5,467 feet per second—over a mile a second—a force more than sufficient for its tungsten core to penetrate 9.5 inches of armor at six thousand yards. After the round burns through the outer armor of an enemy tank in mere milliseconds, the tungsten core fragments, sending over a hundred shrapnel particles weighing at least an ounce and six hundred fragments weighing less than an ounce into the interior compartment of the tank. These fragments ricochet against the tank's interior crew compartment at speeds of 3,000 feet per second, sufficient to pierce the bodies of the crew scores of times before spending their velocity.

Another example of the killing capacity of today's tank ammunition is the HEP-T (High Explosive Plastic Tracer) round, which works on a different ballistic principle. The HEP-T weighs fifty-two pounds and has a muzzle velocity of 4,200 feet per second carrying a warhead filled with plastic explosive. When the warhead strikes the target it spreads out in a blob of plastic the size of a dinner plate and is detonated by a fuse. The explosion does not penetrate the armor, but leaves a large dent as the explosive force is channeled inward toward the crew compartment. The shock of the explosion is so great that chunks of metal (spall) are blasted away from the interior walls of the tank's crew compartment, sending the fragments into the crew's bodies at speeds greater than the speed of sound. There are no tanks in the world which can ensure the survivability of their crews when hit with an APDS or HEP-T round. Everyone always dies.

The greater killing power of tanks has increased the need for the infantry to improve its own mobility. In the offensive, infantry has to be mounted in armored vehicles to keep up with the rapid advance of the tanks. The result is the armored personnel carrier (APC). Today, one of every two U.S. infantrymen rides into battle in an APC. The number of armored personnel carriers in the Soviet Army is thirty-seven times as great as it was in World War II. War on wheels has arrived.

To be sure squeezing ten infantrymen into a single APC has its disadvantages. A single antitank round into an APC will kill at least 70 percent of its occupants and wound the remaining 30 percent. Placing so many infantrymen into one target area has increased the probability of multiple kills for tank and missile gunners. On the other hand, the APC has increased the killing power of the infantry many times over since World War II. A single M-113A APC carries thirteen combat troops and mounts a fifty-caliber machine gun with two thousand rounds of ammunition on the vehicle's cupola. It can also mount two M-60 machine guns, each capable of firing a thousand rounds a minute. Its ability to carry ammunition is far greater than a World War II truck. With a complete load, it can carry 3,570 rounds of fifty-caliber ammunition, 8,400 rounds of M-60 ammunition, 5,050 rounds of rifle ammunition, 144 40mm grenades, four Claymore mines, ten antitank missiles and their launchers. It is a piece of battlefield machinery that simply did not exist in World War II.

The infantry fighting vehicle (IFV) has added yet another dimension to the killing power of the infantry. The American M-3 Bradley is a lightly armored tracked vehicle resembling a large APC. It can carry nine infantrymen into battle. But its real killing power lies in its weaponry. The M-3 mounts either a 25mm chain gun or the 37mm Bushmaster automatic cannon. The Bushmaster can fire either armor-piercing or high-explosive ammunition at a rate of almost a thousand rounds a minute. It carries a 7.2mm machine gun and a dual TOW antitank missile launcher with seven missiles. Its turret stabilization system allows it to fire on the move, and it has a fully computerized fire control system with a full complement of imaging sights.

Infantry fighting vehicles can be employed in many ways. By far the most common is to use an APC as a missile-firing antitank platform or as a missile- or gun-firing air defense platform. The advent of the APC and its variants has revolutionized warfare since it places in the hands of the infantry a mobility and firepower, including the ability to kill tanks and aircraft, that was nonexistent in World War II. The problem, of course, is that the other side has similar weaponry with the same capabilities. Once again technology has increased the intensity and lethality of war.

Helicopters and Strike Aircraft

Nowhere has the impact of military technology been felt more than in the introduction of two major airborne weapons systems, the strike aircraft and the armed helicopter. In World War II, the P-47 ground-support airplane could fly a hundred miles to its target, stay over it for less than thirty minutes, and deliver only machine-gun fire and two 250-pound bombs. Today, the A-10 Warthog, specifically designed as a close-support and tank-killing aircraft, can fly two hundred and fifty miles to its target, loiter over the area for two hours, and carry over 16,000 pounds of bombs, more than the bomb load of a World War II B-29 Superfortress. In addition, the A-10 carries a 30mm seven-barreled rotating gun cluster in its nose capable of firing armor-piercing and high-explosive shells each the size of a milk bottle. The gun can fire 4,200 rounds per minute. A two-second burst fires 135 rounds into a target. The high-explosive round, thanks to the wonders of modern chemistry, produces an explosive force six times that of a 20mm shell. Its armor-piercing round with its warhead of depleted uranium metal produces fourteen times the kinetic energy impact of a 20mm shell and can penetrate all known thicknesses of tank armor plate. A two-second burst is sufficient to kill a tank several times over.

Another awesome ground-support aircraft is the C-130H Spectre. Originally designed to locate and kill forces hiding in dense jungle, the Spectre truly fulfills the promise of its motto, "death from above." The Spectre is equipped with four 20mm Vulcan cannons with six barrels, each cannon capable of firing 6,000 rounds per minute. It also carries four 7.62mm multi-barreled miniguns which can fire at 10,000 rounds per minute and a 40mm Bofors cannon capable of 2,000 rounds per minute. As if to add more death to injury, the Spectre also mounts a 105mm automatic howitzer! The Spectre's purpose is to deliver death from above quickly and silently. Accordingly, all its guns are linked to automatic electronic and infrared detection devices. Its on-board electronics enable it to "see" an enemy hidden in multiple layers of jungle canopy and automatically direct its guns on the target, so that a single pass is often fatal to the enemy below. With all its guns firing at once, the Spectre is capable of reducing all the buildings in a city block to rubble in less than one minute. Captured Vietcong troops who had experienced an attack by the Spectre testify that it is an experience they are never likely to forget.

Close air support is, of course, only one role for modern strike aircraft. They are also expected to be able to engage enemy aircraft and destroy them and to interdict enemy forces massing hundreds of miles behind the front. A new generation of air-to-air missiles has revolutionized aerial combat. The AIM-9 Sidewinder, for example, can seek and destroy enemy aircraft up to ten miles away. Its kill-per-engagement record is 92 percent. The A-54 Phoenix missile can be launched from up to a hundred miles from its target. During the last ten miles of its flight, it is automatically guided by its own homing radar. Its kill-to-engagement record is 90 percent. In short, it is now possible for aircraft to kill each other from distances well beyond the range of sight. Moreover, unlike earlier heat-seeking missiles, modern missiles need not be fired from behind the target. They may approach it with equal lethality from any direction, including head-on.

While missiles have an aura of high tech it is important not to forget the "ordinary" bomb. However, compared to the TNT bombs of World War II, today's bombs are anything but ordinary. A cluster of modern conventional bombs can produce the same explosive effect as low-yield nuclear weapons. Since the war in Vietnam—where we dropped thirty-six tons of bombs for every square mile of both North and South Vietnam—the improvements in the effectiveness of aircraft-delivered bombs has been amazing. Bombs have become more compact and slender, allowing more explosive to be carried. Of course, the explosives themselves are many times as powerful as the TNT filler of the good old days. They have also become far more accurate due to a number of devices ranging from tail retarding devices to optical and laser guidance systems.

Bombs are also more versatile. They can be used to carry rather ordinary chemical munitions like white phosphorus, which can only be stopped from burning entirely through the body by putting the affected limb underwater while a surgeon picks out the pieces of phosphorus. They can also deliver a full range of chemical munitions like mustard and nerve gas. They are cheap and effective. A simple cluster bomb, no larger than an old-fashioned 250-pound bomb, can carry within its casing hundreds of smaller bomblets. Where before there had been a single explosion, there are now hundreds of smaller explosions, vastly increasing the number of shrapnel shards that can slice through a soldier's flesh. A single cluster bomb has the same effect as 600 well-aimed World War II 81mm mortar rounds impacting at once! Few soldiers can be expected to survive such an attack. If the shrapnel doesn't get them, the concussion will.

The Fuel Air Munition (FAM) bombs offer a new wrinkle. These bombs carry an explosive liquid—propane, butane, propylene oxide, etc.—which is released in a dense cloud over a battlefield. The cloud is highly combustible. When detonated by a delayed fuse carried in the bomb's base, the explosion produces five times the force of an equivalent amount of TNT. Thus a 250-pound FAM has the explosive equivalent of a 1,200-pound bomb. Three 100-pound FAMs produce a combustible cloud fifty-six feet across by nine feet thick. Upon detonation, the cloud produces an explosive combustive effect greater than that of a low-yield nuclear weapon. Another bomb, the Daisy Cutter of Vietnam lineage, creates a blast overpressure of 1,000 pounds per square inch, a force equivalent to a man being hit with a baseball bat over every square inch of his body. In Vietnam, Daisy Cutters killed earthworms one hundred yards from the center of the crater.

Battlefield helicopters have revolutionized the mobility of combat forces. Compared to World War II, the mobility of antitank forces mounted on helicopters has increased almost twenty times while the ability to move troop units about the battlefield has increased more than one hundred times. More than any other invention the helicopter is responsible for the new dimensions of war—the deep and rear battles. Within minutes troops with their full complement of weaponry can now be ferried deep into the enemy's rear. They can also be inserted in the path of advancing enemy forces miles to the front of the line. No such capacity existed for World War II commanders. Besides the obvious ability of helicopters to ferry troops and carry cargo—a medium-lift helicopter can carry twice the cargo of a World War II "deuce and a half" truck at five times the speed—the most important role of the helicopter is in troop and tank attack.

Attack helicopters can fly close to the ground and surprise tanks and troops. The helicopter provides a much more stable, thus more accurate, missile and gun platform than other aircraft, can approach within much closer ranges, bring a greater variety of weapons to bear, and do so for much longer periods of time than a fixed-wing strike aircraft. Helicopters such as the A-1 Cobra are equipped with the M-28 chin turret which can carry two 7.62mm miniguns or two 40mm grenade launchers which fire 450 grenades per minute over a range of 2,000 yards. Each grenade has a lethal radius of ten yards. The Cobra can also be fitted with two M-200 stanchion rocket pods each holding nineteen 2.75-inch rockets. In one configuration, the Cobra can carry fifty-four rockets. The 2.75-inch Tiny Tim rocket has an explosive force equal to that of an 81mm mortar shell. Those rockets equipped with white phosphorus heads equal the explosive force of the 4.2-inch (107mm) mortar shell. The killing power of these systems is enhanced greatly by their linkage to a full array of electronic sighting and computerized aiming devices which hold the guns on target no matter what maneuvering position the helicopter itself is in.

In the antitank role helicopters are indeed awesome weapons. A single Cobra can carry eight TOW antitank missiles, generally regarded as the best antitank missiles in the world. The TOW's killing range is 4,687 yards. Its shaped explosive charge warhead is capable of piercing any known thickness of tank armor, leaving holes two feet in diameter in a tank's hull. A TOW's optical sight is so good that at a thousand yards a tank fills the sight screen. Once fired, the missile is guided to its target at a speed of 368 miles an hour.

The AH-64 Apache helicopter is even more deadly as a tank killer. It can carry sixteen TOW missiles or sixteen of the new Hellfire missiles. The Hellfire is a third-generation missile and incorporates a true "fire and forget" homing device. The helicopter aims the missile, fires it, and can then take evasive action with no need to remain on station for three or four seconds to guide the missile to its target. The Apache also mounts nineteen 2.75-inch rockets and a Hughes 30mm chain gun in its nose. It too is equipped with the full complement of computers and electronic gunsights. Pilots are equipped with a new helmet "killer sight." As the pilot turns his head and eyes to look at a target, the guns automatically follow his head and eye movements. Thus, to see the target is to hit it and, in general, to hit the target is to kill it.

The helicopter, more than any other weapon, is responsible for the "swirling tactics" that will characterize modern war. The ability of a commander to strike far to his front or deep in his enemy's rear means, of course, that he must be able to counter similar tactics on the part of his enemy. Thus, there are no more safe areas. Tanks may now be struck hundreds of miles from the fighting zone as they are loaded onto railway cars for the journey to the front. Staff headquarters hundreds of miles from the front may be hit. Hospitals, once safely in the rear, along with port areas, airfields, communications stations, road junctions, and other strategically important areas, are now equally vulnerable. So important has the helicopter become that the Soviets have configured their helicopters with weapons designed to shoot down Allied helicopters on tank-killing missions. The next war may well witness the birth of helicopter-to-helicopter aerial combat.

Chemical Weapons

The one factor which may influence the modern battlefield most dramatically of all, and one for which there are no meaningful ways to determine its impact, is the use of chemical weapons. These may turn out to be the most deadly means for killing and incapacitating troops in the next war. In the words of one U.S. Army report, "if their use is not inhibited, they could swing the balance in a conventional war."

The first large-scale use of chemical weapons occurred in World War I on April 22, 1915, at Ypres, Belgium, when the German Army released the contents of five thousand canisters of chlorine gas. The victims, two French elite divisions, were taken by surprise, broke, and ran, opening a five-mile gap in the Allied line. After Ypres, chemical munitions were used more and more frequently by all sides. The last year of the war, 1918, saw more chemical weapons used than in the preceding three years. Approximately 1.3 million gas casualties were inflicted in World War I, about 92,000 of which were fatal. No less than 35 percent of all gas casualties, most of them fatalities, were inflicted against Russian troops, a fact which no doubt accounts for the present Soviet interest in producing and defending against chemical weapons. Those who believe that such weapons are too horrible to be used again ought to remember that the American plan for the invasion of Japan in World War II called for the large-scale use of chemical weapons against civilians to reduce Allied ground casualties. Moreover, the Japanese used chemical weapons frequently against Chinese soldiers and civilians in their attack on China before World War II. Since World War II, chemical weapons have been used in

Vietnam, Cambodia, Yemen, Iran, Iraq, and Afghanistan. In the minds of most military commanders, chemical weapons are just one more weapon of war whose use is expected and planned for.

Today the Soviet Army is fully configured to fight with chemical weapons. Special units, with no fewer than 100,000 troops, are designed to attack with and defend against chemical weapons. The Soviets have sixteen different chemical delivery systems, ranging from aircraft bombs and artillery shells to chemical grenades and land mines. In addition, most of their battlefield vehicles are designed to operate in a chemical environment—unlike U.S. vehicles—and their soldiers are issued protective suits. What makes the Soviet chemical threat so likely to be used is that American chemical capabilities, offensive and defensive, are almost nonexistent. Moreover, chemical weapons are much more effective when used on the offensive, and seizing and maintaining the offensive is the key element in Soviet combat doctrine. The range of chemical weapons staggers the imagination. Such weapons range from simple gas compounds, like mustard gas, to blood and nerve agents for which no real defense exists.

While the use of chemical agents may well kill hundreds of thousands of soldiers—to say nothing of the helpless civilians trapped in or near the fighting who have no means of protecting themselves—the major impact of chemical attacks is likely to be psychiatric. And a soldier who is out of action because of psychiatric breakdown is just as useless as a soldier who has been shot. The psychiatric impact of chemical weapons is hard for the average civilian to comprehend. For example, a British Army study conducted in 1921 found that of the 600,000 Allied gas casualties in World War I, no fewer than 400,000 were psychiatric in origin or self-inflicted. Frightened soldiers would use a small stick to pick up some residue of mustard gas and apply it on their skin. Once the blisters appeared, they would report to the battalion aid station and get out of the fighting for a short while. In another study done in 1927 the American Army found that two of every three men who reported to an aid station complaining of gas symptoms had not even been exposed to a gas attack! Most were suffering the symptoms of chemical exposure but their cause was psychosomatic.

In a modern war soldiers on all sides forced to don chemical protection suits would almost certainly suffer a very high rate of psychiatric collapse within a few hours. Modern chemical suits simply don't work very well. On average, the suit must be changed every ten hours to ensure that chemical residues do not penetrate it. They are made of a rubberized material and are very hot. At 65 degrees, a soldier cannot function in a suit for more than three hours. His combat efficiency is reduced by at least 50 percent and as much as 80 percent. One U.S. estimate is that simply putting on the suit reduces the combat effectiveness of troops by 50 percent. Worse, the soldier's head is encased in a mask which makes it very difficult to see when the lenses become fogged. His ability to hear and communicate declines by over 80 percent and he is subject to rapid heat exhaustion. Nor can he take off the suit to gain relief. Once a chemical alert is sounded, there are few reliable ways to determine what chemicals have been used or how long they will pose a danger. Some agents last six months or longer. Others, such as blood and nerve agents, are colorless, odorless, and tasteless and only a few can be detected by electronic sensors. In many cases the only sure way to determine if the area is safe is to coax a soldier out of his suit and see if he dies!

The soldier is therefore trapped inside his chemical suit psychologically and physically isolated from his comrades. All he can be aware of is the throb of his own pulse, his rapid breathing, and the smell of his own sweat. To make matters worse, many of the initial signs of chemical poisoning—rapid heartbeat, sweating, shortness of breath, etc.— are exactly those associated with the normal physiological stress reactions of battle. Isolated from his comrades, the soldier in a chemical suit is forced to deal with his physical symptoms alone. Who can blame him if he misinterprets his symptoms as chemically induced and suffers psychiatric collapse? If he believes he has been exposed, the soldier is likely to inject himself with atropine, a chemical which, at best, is a poor antidote against chemical attack. The problem is that once he injects himself, the atropine reaction visits a terrible set of symptoms upon his body. Common effects of atropine injection are dehydration, incoherency, and mental disorientation, all severe enough to render the soldier useless. The mere suspicion that a unit may have been subjected to a chemical attack is enough in most cases to generate a very high rate of psychiatric casualties. In World War I, for example, chemical weapons produced four times as many nonfatal battle casualties as were produced by regular explosive weapons and most of these were psychiatric.

The ability of fear to debilitate soldiers under chemical conditions cannot be overestimated. In 1985, a battalion of the French Foreign Legion was undergoing a mock chemical attack at its base in Corsica. This unit had been through this exercise many times before. Usually, a single aircraft would pass low over the troops and drop water vapor, simulating a gas attack. This time, however, the instructors replaced the water vapor with a harmless red powder that the troops had never seen. Once the aircraft released the powder, the seasoned troops of the Legion were shaken to the core. The whole battalion, apparently believing that some horrible mistake had been made and that real chemical compounds had been used, simply came apart. Scores of soldiers writhed on the ground manifesting all the symptoms of a genuine chemical attack. Some almost died from their psychologically generated symptoms. The rest either panicked and ran or froze on the spot expecting to die. While there are no reliable means for predicting the number of physical or psychological casualties that will result from an actual attack, there is widespread agreement that the results will be catastrophic. It is fully expected that the World War I psychiatric casualty rates will be greatly exceeded.

The Poor Bloody Infantry

Since the sixteenth century the infantry has suffered the greatest number of casualties in any war. Dubbed the "queen of battle" by military commanders, to those who served in it, it has always been "the poor bloody infantry." While modern weaponry has increased the infantry's ability to kill by several thousand times since the sixteenth century, it is surely true that human beings have remained essentially the same for at least the last two hundred thousand years. Certainly we have evolved no mechanisms, biological or psychological, which have made us any more able to withstand the killing and maiming effects of weaponry; nor is there any evidence that we are any more able to withstand the psychological impact that the horror of war has always had upon soldiers. The weaponry has changed dramatically; the soldiers have remained the same.

The individual infantryman now has at his disposal weapons of much greater destruction than did his predecessors. A single infantryman now possesses the means to shoot down aircraft or kill tanks. But the truth is that the exponential increase in firepower and lethality of other weapons has simply not been matched by either the firepower of the infantry's weapons or, more importantly, the ability to escape the lethal effects of other weapons. What this all adds up to is that the infantry soldier is more vulnerable than ever. Infantrymen will die in windrows in a modern war much as they have in wars past.

All of which raises the question of casualties. Modern conventional war has become so destructive that neither side has been able to come up with realistic casualty figures as to how many dead, wounded, and psychiatrically broken men would result from even a single day's battle, let alone a long war. U.S. military commanders freely admit that their estimates of 920 men per day per division—about a 6 percent loss rate a day—are probably incorrect since they are based upon computer models which are rooted largely in assumptions drawn from World War II experience.

The one example of two modern conventional armies at war occurred in the 1973 Arab-Israeli war. Both sides suffered losses of 50 percent in men and equipment in less than two weeks of fighting. But the 1973 war is not instructive for accurately calculating casualties in a modern conventional conflict. For one thing, the size of the forces was nowhere near what it would be in a battle in Central Europe and, equally important, there have been numerous improvements and new weapons since then. A 50 percent loss rate in two weeks can only be regarded as the most optimistic case for predicting casualties in a future conventional war. Even assuming this "best case" scenario, the number of men killed and wounded in a Central European battle would approximate two million on both sides if the battle lasted only two weeks.

At least the dead will be dead, but what about the wounded? The simple fact of the matter is that neither side has sufficient medical resources to deal with the massive numbers of wounded soldiers that would result from a conventional war. For example, the U.S. military has only about half the number of doctors it had in service during the Vietnam War to deal with wounded casualties that will occur at four to five times the rate in much shorter periods of time. There are only 149 anesthesiologists available for wartime requirements and only 420 surgeons. Fewer than 2,000 beds would be available to treat the wounded in Europe, which means that we would have to evacuate our wounded directly to the United States for treatment. Such a prospect, which is official military doctrine, assumes that the aircraft and the airfields from which such evacuations would be staged will be available, a doubtfully valid assumption given the nature of modern war. In every test done on evacuation capability, the United States has found that it simply does not have the aircraft and crews to evacuate large numbers of casualties. Moreover, given the time it takes to evacuate casualties over such long distances, it is expected that 20 percent of the wounded will die needlessly as a result of delayed treatment over the long trip. It seems a foregone conclusion that only the lightly wounded will survive. The rest will die.

Then there are those who will be driven mad by the fighting. In a modern war the chances of becoming a psychiatric casualty are more than twice as great as being killed by enemy fire. And even this prediction is drawn from historical experience and cannot be made with accuracy. A few years ago the U.S. Army attempted to measure just how intense the modern battlefield would be compared to World War II. They found that in World War II, heavy combat produced an exposure to enemy "combat pulses"—ground attacks, artillery shelling, aircraft bombing, etc.—at a rate of two to four a day. Today, the enemy as well as Western forces are expected to deliver twelve to fourteen combat pulses a day! Thus, modern conventional war is likely to be anywhere from four to seven times as intense as World War II combat.

The impact of this level of battle intensity upon the ability of the soldier to retain his sanity is tremendous. If one were to extrapolate the increases in firepower and lethality of today back to World War II, the number of psychiatric casualties suffered only by the American ground forces in that war would jump from 241,960 to 967,840 at a minimum. But firepower and lethality are not the only factors which increase the probabilities and rates at which soldiers will become debilitated by psychiatric stress. Other factors, paradoxically, are even more important.

Psychiatric stress casualties increase greatly when the soldier feels isolated. Clearly, the need to fight in chemical suits or from within armored personnel carriers where one shot can kill all the men on board will increase psychological isolation. Increased physical fatigue strongly affects psychiatric casualty rates. Since the soldier will have to fight longer and harder, often cut off from his supply lines, psychiatric debilitation rates can be expected to rise even further. The need to fight at night will generate even higher rates, as will the need for an almost constant stream of replacements, which will weaken the social cohesion of the combat group, and which is the first line of defense against psychiatric breakdown. Finally, the huge increases in indirect fire upon the troops will generate extremely high rates of psychiatric casualties.

Both the intensity and the nature of modern conventional war are likely to generate rates of psychiatric casualties never before seen in warfare. Again using a World War II model with constant manpower rates, if the factors associated with modern war were operative at that time, the number of psychiatric casualties would have reached one million, an increase of almost five times the actual World War II rate! It is highly probable that the rate of psychiatric casualties in a modern conventional war will account for almost 50 percent of the total manpower loss on both sides. It is, at best, highly questionable whether any army could long sustain such rates and survive.

Conclusion

What this brief sketch of modern conventional war should make obvious is that war is no longer a rational means to gain political ends. War has become an activity that has surpassed the ability of human beings to endure it. An army sent off to war, even if victorious, will return a bedraggled, maimed mob of madmen. Whatever proportionality between means and ends that may have once existed on the field of battle no longer exists. Even the victors must pass through a slaughterhouse on the way to victory.

War is no longer tolerable to the human mind. We have reached a point where almost everyone exposed to combat will, within a comparatively short time, be killed, wounded, or driven mad. Indeed, the greatest threat to the modern soldier is neither death nor being wounded. It is the threat of being psychiatrically debilitated from mental breakdown. In such circumstances, one can only wonder what meaning such human qualities as courage, endurance, and heroism still have. On a battlefield when large numbers of men are slaughtered for no greater reason than that they were in the wrong place at the wrong time, one can only wonder of what worth military expertise and training are. When so many are killed and maimed so quickly, of what value is the notion of personal sacrifice?

What is clear is that most civilians have no idea what they are in for once called to the colors of their country to do battle. Certainly their experiences will far surpass anything they could have remotely imagined. Many of them will be driven mad and some will never recover from it. Yet, with all the emphasis on the technology of war, its cost in terms of dollars, and the frequency with which it penetrates our consciousness, for most people the thought of being driven mad by combat never enters their minds. How strange this is since madness in war has been one of the few constants that have accompanied soldiers from earliest times. And there is every evidence that it will be an even more prevalent companion of those who take the field of battle the next time.

2

War and Madness

To understand the development of war is to recognize a single indisputable fact: not only is war becoming more lethal in terms of its ability to kill and maim but it is far more destructive in its ability to drive soldiers mad. Indeed, as the warriors among us improve the technology of killing, the power to drive combatants crazy, to debilitate them through fear and mental collapse, is growing at an even faster rate.

There seems to be a tendency in modern man to regard the past as somehow more idyllic than it was and to endow it with the quality of a golden age in which many of the human problems men now face were somehow absent or not as important. Lieutenant Colonel Lawrence Ingraham and Major Frederick Manning, both members of the staff of the Department of Military Psychiatry at the Walter Reed Army Institute of Research, have written that "psychiatric battle casualties are a phenomenon new with 20th-century warfare."[1] Accounts of past battles seem so often to offer examples of individual heroism and courage and all too seldom report acts of cowardice and fear. It is as if we were the first generation to question our ability to endure the horror of battle. At the very least, military histories seem to simplify all aspects of battle—perhaps a virtue of hindsight—so that the complications which are always attendant upon modern war are often absent or minimized in accounts of wars past. One result is to convey the impression that men who fought in earlier times were somehow different from those who will fight the battles of the future. This seems especially so in accounts of performance and endurance under fire. Nothing could be further from the truth.

Fear and madness have been man's companions in war since the beginning of recorded history and, most probably, before that. There is clear evidence that men recognized early on that the ability to conquer fear was crucial in achieving victory over one's enemies. Xenophon, himself an experienced soldier and troop commander, wrote almost 2,500 years ago that "I am sure that not numbers or strength bring victory in war; but whichever army goes into battle stronger in its soul."[2] There is no good reason to believe that soldiers in past times were any less fearful of dying or being maimed than their modern-day counterparts. Moreover, that battle has driven men of the past just as mad as it has driven modern-day soldiers seems a historical fact. Further, the forms that madness has taken in the past are identical to the forms with which it has afflicted modern soldiers. The ability of armies and their medical corps to identify these symptoms as madness has changed greatly over the years, as have the names which military physicians have assigned to them. The willingness of modern armies to tolerate such symptoms has also changed. What has not changed is that battle drives a considerable number of its participants crazy.

From as far back as ancient Egypt, we have written accounts that testify to the fear that men must endure in battle. In a letter written almost three thousand years ago, an Egyptian combat veteran, Hori, writes to an inexperienced young officer: "You determine to go forward. . . . Shuddering seizes you, the hair of your head stands on end, your soul lies in your hand."[3] The importance of fear in deciding military battles cannot be underestimated. Until the nineteenth century battles were usually settled fairly quickly, commonly in less than a single day. As a rule, such battles were normally not decided by the amount of killing and wounding, which was almost always considerable on both sides. What decided battles most often was fear and panic. Usually after a short period of engagement—often minutes or hours—one side broke and ran, leaving the other to pursue and slaughter it. In an age of primitive weaponry with limited range the human factor was paramount in the equation of combat effectiveness. It is, thus, little wonder that the writers of Greece and Rome should spend so much time on the subject in their accounts of military operations.

That men broke and ran was a fact of military life, and it still is. But an experienced commander even then had to have the sensitivity to recognize what Farley Mowatt has called "the worm of fear" in his men and to take steps to prevent their succumbing to it. In 480 B.C., Leonidas was in command of a force of Spartan soldiers whose task was to defend the pass of Thermopylae. As an astute commander he recognized that some of his troops had been shaken in earlier action and were likely to break completely if engaged again. Herodotus, the Greek historian, records that Leonidas "dismissed them when he realized that they had no heart for the fight and were unwilling to take their share of the danger."[4] Here is a clear example of the fact that early commanders recognized that units can become emotionally exhausted and that when they do they are at risk of breaking down. Then, as now, the only solution to the problem was to pull the men from the line. Since World War I it has been common practice in all armies of the West to rotate combat soldiers and units out of the line on regular schedules in order to prevent them from collapsing and becoming psychiatric casualties. Every modern commander is trained in military schools to recognize the signs that a unit is near its emotional limits and to understand that from such men nothing further can reasonably be asked. It is a stark reality of war that men have limits of psychological endurance.

If fear has been a constant companion in war, so has madness. Even a cursory reading of the accounts of battles over the ages provides numerous examples of men manifesting various forms of psychiatric and emotional symptoms brought on by the fear and stress of war. Today we recognize such symptoms for what they are and call them "combat reactions." Their occurrence was as well known to soldiers of earlier times as to the modern soldier, although their dynamics were not understood. History illustrates how remarkably consistent the occurrence of battle reactions has been.

Herodotus records that as the battle for the pass of Thermopylae was about to begin, two soldiers of the handpicked elite Spartan unit of three hundred reported to the surgeon and claimed that they were suffering from an "acute inflammation of the eyes." That two soldiers should acquire the same ailment at the precise point when the fighting was about to start is, to say the least, suspicious. The soldiers asked for permission to retire to the rear. When the battle began one of the Spartan soldiers, Aristodemus, "finding his heart failed him," remained safely in the rear and did not join the fight, although the other soldier did. After the battle, the Spartans gave Aristodemus the name "the trembler" for his refusal to fight and Aristodemus "found himself in such disgrace that he hanged himself."[5] Studies of soldiers in World Wars I and II demonstrate clearly that they often suffered psychosomatically induced ailments prior to an engagement and often used it as an excuse to avoid combat. Indeed, one of the major tasks of today's unit psychiatrist is to distinguish such stress-induced ailments from genuine ones. It is also evident from prior studies that some soldiers who succeed in evading combat through a contrived illness—although they may not always consciously know it is contrived—sometimes have great difficulty coming to grips with their emotions. This seems more so when the unit to which they belong meets disaster, as the Spartans did at Thermopylae. As in the case of Aristodemus, soldiers with similar experiences often suffer severe depression or psychosis and, all too often, commit suicide. There is nothing in the story of Aristodemus that would be unfamiliar to a psychiatrist who dealt with psychiatric casualties in World War II or Vietnam.

In another instance, Plutarch notes that in the Roman siege of Syracuse in 211 B.C., in which Archimedes, the great Greek inventor and mathematician was killed, a number of the Greek soldiers defending the city "were stricken dumb with terror."[6] If we may take Plutarch literally, he is surely recording an example of the psychiatric condition called surdomutism, an inability to speak induced by great fear. Russian psychiatrists stationed at the front in the Russo-Japanese War of 1905 were the first to clinically diagnose this condition as resulting directly from the trauma of battle stress. In World Wars I and II the Russians saw countless occurrences of the same condition. They developed a method—the Kaufmann method of strong electrical shock—to deal with it. Surdomutism was diagnosed by American, British, and French doctors in World War I and it occurred in World War II as well, although apparently with somewhat less frequency. Today it is recognized as a common, though serious, conversion reaction to the stress of battle.

Roman military medicine made its institutional appearance during the Punic Wars (264–146 B.C.). The removal of the wounded and shocked from the battle to hospitals located in cities and ports far to the rear was difficult. The trip to the hospitals was often long and rugged and many of the wounded died before they reached medical help. Then, as now, medical evacuation to the rear was likely to make more difficult the task of returning the slightly wounded soldier to his unit, as the slightly wounded were often mistakenly evacuated as well. The Romans established a series of military hospitals staffed by Greek physicians along the roads leading to the battle, thus introducing a major principle of modern military medicine, the principle of proximity of treatment. Evacuation of the wounded was accomplished more or less the way it is done today, with the most severely wounded given the last priority of movement while the less severe cases were treated as close to the battle as possible. The principle of Roman military medicine was the same as that which guides modern military medicine and psychiatry: to return as many men as quickly as possible to the battle. Over time, the Romans established a network of military hospitals that extended throughout the empire.

One result of this institutionalized and permanent military medical system was the compiling of excellent records of wounds suffered by Roman soldiers. And among these records, as expected, there are examples of conditions which were brought on by combat stress. Among the most interesting of these are the records dealing with self-inflicted wounds. Polybius, the Greek military historian, records that as early as 168 B.C. the Romans were familiar with soldiers who deliberately injured themselves in order to avoid battle. The problem must have been of some importance, because this highly bureaucratized permanent army published in its standing regulations the punishment for self-inflicted wounds: death.[7] The phenomenon of the self-inflicted wound appears again and again throughout military history and, of course, it appeared in the Vietnam War. In one instance, a medic in Vietnam actually anesthetized the limbs of soldiers who planned to shoot themselves to obtain an honorable discharge for a war-related injury! In World War II a ring of sergeants at embarkation ports were arrested for selling instructions to new recruits on how to escape being shipped out. One of the recommended ways was to "accidentally" shoot oneself in the foot! Psychiatrists now recognize that many of the "accidents" involving soldiers about to go to war are in reality "secondary reactions" to fear and stress.

Another category of "accident" occurs when the soldier is so emotionally fatigued that he can no longer process mental information. High incidents of trench foot and frostbite in a unit are regarded by the American Army as clear signs of emotional stress approaching breakdown. Interestingly, frostbite almost always occurs on the hand that the soldier uses to pull the trigger. Whether the Romans were familiar with such a range of stress reactions is unclear. That they had to deal with the problem of self-inflicted wounds is beyond dispute.

An interesting account of an acute fear reaction which produced debilitating symptoms that made further military action impossible is found in the *Anglo-Saxon Chronicle*, which recounts a battle in 1003 between English and Danish armies. The English commander, Aelfric, leading his men toward the enemy, suddenly became violently ill and began to vomit. He was so sick that he couldn't continue and the Danes easily routed their adversaries. It may be that Aelfric had previously suffered from this condition in similar circumstances, for the *Chronicle* notes that "he was up to his old tricks" and that Aelfric "once again betrayed the people whom he should have led."[8] That fear in battle or just before it can cause symptomatic reactions that can debilitate a soldier is also clear from studies during and since World War II. In a study of American soldiers assigned to a combat division in France in 1944, over half admitted that they became sick to their stomachs, felt faint, lost control of their bowels (thus the old adage, "scared shitless"), or broke out in cold sweats during battle. About a third reported that these symptoms had a significant effect on their ability to carry out their duties.[9] Almost all of us have had some direct experience with this feeling of illness induced by fear. Many athletes vomit before a game. Anyone who has felt weakness in the knees from witnessing the carnage of an auto accident or the paralyzing adrenaline rush that results from a near-miss on the highway understands what Aelfric felt.

In 1346 on the field of Crécy a unit of Genoese bowmen

simply came apart under stress. They had marched all day and were physically worn out. Their commander told the king that "they were not in a fit condition to do any great things that day in battle."[10] Despite this warning, they were committed to battle first. They engaged in a small skirmishing action, and when they were subject to counterfire from the enemy, they completely collapsed and "some of them cut the strings of their crossbows" (no doubt the medieval equivalent of the jammed rifle of later years), "others flung them on the ground, and all turned about and retreated."[11] Modern experience has clearly taught that fatigued troops—hungry, thirsty, tired—will very readily break under even moderate stress. It has also taught us that there are objective limits to human endurance that cannot be exceeded; the only treatment is rest and relief from the line.

One interesting aspect of combat-reaction symptoms is the "million-dollar wound," or "blighty," a term apparently coined during World War I but reflecting a reality that is much older. Soldiers exposed to battle almost all wish to escape the horror (about 2 percent seem to enjoy it!). But a number of "myths" that function to protect the ego demand that some "legitimate" way be found to gain relief. A legitimate escape is one that will not be seen as cowardice by one's peers, family, or friends. The "million-dollar wound" is a physical injury not severe enough to be life-threatening or even physically debilitating at the time it is inflicted, but is a wound that provides an adequate excuse to gain relief from the battlefield. Once wounded, however slightly, most combat soldiers feel that they have done their share and have honorably earned the right to be removed from the fight. In the siege of Constantinople in 1453 there was at least one soldier who understood the usefulness of such a wound.

Captain John Justiniani commanded a unit in defense of a section of the city wall. From all accounts he and his unit had fought well throughout the day. But near the end of the day Justiniani was slightly wounded in the hand by an arrow. He immediately left his post to seek a surgeon. The Emperor Palaeologus, who was acting as commander-in-chief of the defense of the city, saw Justiniani leave his post and ran to intercept him on his way to the rear. The emperor entreated him not to retire, for "the danger is pressing." Justiniani, trembling with fear, refused to be stopped and continued his flight to the rear even though his wound was minor and was not disabling.[12] As is often the case in modern war, men will fight well until given an excuse by circumstance—a slight wound is a perfect excuse—to leave the fight. During Custer's last battle, for example, soldiers under Major Marcus Reno's command, surrounded and under attack for two days, left their defensive positions for the medical station with minor injuries even though it offered no cover and was exposed continuously to hostile fire and was no safer—and perhaps considerably less so—than positions at the perimeter of the battle.

Almost anyone who has served a stint in military service in almost any army (and, no doubt, at almost any time in history) has received what is known as a "Dear John" letter. Sometimes—and the frequency clearly increases when men are at war—a soldier who has received a "Dear John" or in some other way learns that he has lost his girlfriend or wife to another man—safe in the rear area—will become despondent and succumb to a stress-related illness. Some men will deliberately place themselves at risk to the point of overtly courting death. Such men are really committing suicide. Lord Falkland seems to have been just such a case at the battle of Newbury in November 1643. As a chronicler of the battle notes, Falkland, "being there, and having nothing to do, decided to charge; as the two armies were engaging, rode like a madman (as he was) between them, and was shot. . . . Some would needs have the reason of this mad action of throwing away his life. It was the grief of the death of Mrs. Moray . . . who was his mistress and whom he loved above all creatures."[13] Farley Mowatt, in his account of his own battle experiences in Italy in World War

II, recounts the story of a soldier in his unit who received a "Dear John" letter and also squandered his life in similar fashion. Mowatt also recounts that his father had told him the same thing happened to men in his unit in World War I.[14] While many things will cause despondency among men in war, studies of psychiatric casualties in the Vietnam War indicate that a "Dear John" letter is often a major element in precipitating "nostalgia"-related emotional problems.

The stress of war can make itself felt in a number of physical ways. Lord de Ros recorded an interesting incident of battle-stress symptoms involving the Czar of Russia, Peter the Great. At the sack of the city of Narva in 1704, Peter's officers apparently lost control of their men and they began a bloody slaughter of the civilians of the town. Although Peter ordered the slaughter stopped, the troops were in such a frenzy that it continued unabated. Finally, in an act of desperation, the Czar waded into the fray with sword drawn to cut down his own soldiers. He came upon an officer who had literally gone berserk in the slaughter and who, "in the heat of the carnage, was rendered deaf" to his commander's order to stop.[15] Peter killed him with his sword. Examples of men going berserk under fire—a term derived from the drug-induced madness that overtook Viking troops in their battles of the ninth and tenth centuries—are too numerous in modern times to require documentation. This state of extreme physical and psychological excitement made the Viking soldiers capable of acts of great "courage" which often got them killed.

Deafness of soldiers in modern wars has been recognized, at least since the end of World War I, as due far more often to hysterical conversion reactions caused by emotional turbulence than to physiological damage. During World War I, and before that in the American Civil War and the Franco-Prussian War of 1870, deafness in combat soldiers had been explained primarily as a function of concussion and contusion to the brain or eardrums caused by artillery fire. It was this belief which led to the use of the term "shell shock" to explain a number of battle reactions which we now know to be due to emotional turbulence. During World War I hundreds of autopsies were performed on soldiers who had become deaf. Accompanying damage to brain or eardrums was not easily found, a fact which did much to reverse the then current physiological explanations for conversion reactions such as deafness, paralysis, blindness, and surdomutism. Today, whenever such incidents occur among combat soldiers, they are usually treated as emotional and not physical problems.

A particularly interesting reaction to battle stress is found in the way soldiers react to the increased fear of being killed as a consequence of the perceived incompetence of their superiors, usually officers and NCOs. Studies done by the Israeli Defense Force have found that among the most important elements for warding off emotional breakdown in battle—and increasing the battlefield performance of the individual soldier—is the degree to which soldiers trust their officers and believe that they will not squander their men foolishly.[16]

When forced to serve under officers whom they believe to be incompetent and therefore dangerous, soldiers throughout history have resorted to the simple yet effective device of killing them. Assassination involving one of Marlborough's officers at the battle of Gross Hepach in 1704 is a typical example. As one eyewitness recorded the event, an officer, fearing he might be shot by his own men once the battle began, assembled his men and told them that if he survived the day he would mend his ways. After the battle, the officer again called his men together "to call for a cheer." As he took off his hat, he was struck between the eyes with a bullet and "there was decided suspicion that the bullet was no accident."[17]

While there are documented cases of officers being assassinated by their men in World Wars I and II and the Korean War, in the Vietnam War the assassination of officers and sergeants reached major proportions. At least 1,013 documented cases of killing of superiors or attempted killings by fearful troops were reported.[18] In general, the reason behind these assassinations was the fear of officers and NCOs whom the troops perceived to be incompetent or too aggressive or whom they did not trust. Lack of trust was a direct result of a system of individual troop replacement which made it impossible for units to serve together long enough for the men to trust one another. The fact that officers served combat tours of six months while their troops were required to serve "in the bush" for twelve months no doubt also contributed. In any case, killing one's officers as a way of dealing with a terrible fear of what he will cause to be done to the men under him once the shooting starts has a long, if not so noble, history.

During the Spanish siege of Gibraltar in 1727, a soldier who was part of the defense of the city recounted several incidents in his diary that are textbook examples of reactions to combat stress. The soldier records a disciplinary action against another soldier on April 12. The diarist recalls that the soldier was whipped for the fifth time. He had refused to work, fight in defense of the city, or eat and drink.[19] Such symptoms clearly define what later became known as "nostalgia," a psychiatric reaction to stress and fatigue which was reported thousands of times during the American Civil War, World War I, and World War II. During the Vietnam War, American soldiers suffered a comparatively high rate of psychiatric casualties, many of them diagnosed as involving "nostalgia-like" symptoms. In Vietnam, the soldier's emotional turbulence was reflected in a range of symptoms that included alcohol and drug abuse, temporary desertion to a local bar or brothel, and high rates of venereal disease— all regarded by military psychiatrists as secondary symptoms of the stress induced by combat or military life. In extreme cases the soldier's condition can degenerate further to the point where he suffers extreme physical fatigue all the time regardless of how much rest he has had. This is often accompanied by an inability to understand and process even the simplest instructions.

In another entry from the same diarist describing the same battle, he notes that a soldier "withdrew a bit from the fighting line" and inflicted a wound upon himself with his rifle in order to avoid having to continue fighting—an example of the same condition addressed by the Romans and seen by the American Army in Vietnam. Finally, on October 11, an entry records the case of a soldier who quite deliberately put down his rifle, climbed to the belfry of a church steeple, and jumped to his death.[20] Such incidents are well-known reactions to combat stress and they occurred while the city was under siege and great stress was being imposed upon the defenders. These same symptoms emerge again and again in modern wars.

Nostalgia is a cluster of symptoms marked by excessive physical fatigue, an inability to concentrate, an unwillingness to eat or drink leading at times to anorexia, a feeling of isolation and total frustration leading to a general inability to function in a military environment. It was first described by military physicians among Swiss soldiers in 1678.[21] It was also diagnosed among German troops of the same period by German doctors who called the condition *Heimweh* (homesickness). It was thought that the symptoms resulted from the soldier's longing to return home, a very accurate observation confirmed by more modern military psychiatry. French military doctors termed the same symptoms *maladie du pays,* and the Spanish, who noted an outbreak among their soldiers, called it *estar roto* (literally, "to be broken"). Even earlier examples of nostalgia appeared among the soldiers of the Spanish Army of Flanders during the Thirty Years' War. There exists a report from 1643 of soldiers in the Spanish Army being discharged for the same illness. Military physicians recognized even then that the source of the symptoms was emotional and not physical, noting that "imagination alone can cause all this."[22] During the Civil

War autopsies performed on nostalgia patients who died confirmed, however, that nostalgia producing emotional turbulence was quite capable of producing physiological symptoms of disease. Tragically, nostalgia in itself was often fatal, especially if the soldier's emotional resistance was weakened by a wound. When it did not kill, it often drove the soldier to insanity. The recognized cure, then and now, was simply to relieve the soldier from the fighting and send him home on furlough.

Nostalgia was recognized and widely reported during the eighteenth century among the armies of France, Italy, Germany, and Austria. In one instance reported in 1799, a unit of Scottish Highland troops succumbed to the condition almost to a man. All that was needed to trigger the onset of nostalgia, the report notes, was for the Highlanders to hear the sound of bagpipes! Nostalgia was reported among Napoleon's troops at Waterloo and again during the French retreat from Moscow, where the diary of an officer notes numerous incidents of soldiers perishing from the illness as well as being killed because they were unable to defend themselves. In the first year of the American Civil War, 5,213 cases of nostalgia, or 2.34 cases per thousand, were diagnosed.[23] By the end of the war, almost 10,000 cases had been diagnosed among Union soldiers alone. Nostalgia has remained a constant affliction of soldiers; it appeared repeatedly in World Wars I and II. On the basis of one study of psychiatric casualties during the Vietnam War, it seems likely that the major category of war-related neurosis which emerged in that war was nostalgia and its accompanying symptoms.[24]

Sometimes soldiers can develop combat reactions very quickly—indeed, within minutes or even seconds. This type of reaction is called acute battle shock, since the soldier is afflicted with it without having had long periods of exposure to combat which serve to wear down his emotional resistance and invite the onset of reaction symptoms. A classic case of acute battle shock leading to temporary paralysis occurred at the battle of Eylau in 1807. A French officer leading his men in an attack against the Russians had a near-miss when a Russian cannonball ripped by knocking off his shako but without hitting his head. Although the officer was not hit and suffered no head wounds, "I seemed to be blotted out of existence, but I did not fall from my horse. Nevertheless, I could still hear and see, and I preserved all my intellectual faculties, although my limbs were paralyzed to such an extent that I could not move a single finger."[25] While the officer remained paralyzed atop his horse, his unit clashed with the enemy and he was trapped in the middle of the fight. As the only mounted man in an infantry engagement, the experience must have been frightening. The officer was unable to move and lacked even the ability "to press my legs so as to make the animal I rode understand my wish."[26] Eventually, in what must have seemed like hours, the battle moved elsewhere and the officer's horse calmly walked away, taking its paralyzed passenger to safety. The officer "came to his senses" somewhat later and his paralysis abated.

Similar cases of acute hysterical paralysis were common on both sides in World War I and were often accompanied by hysterical stupor. In some incidents the paralysis was localized in the arm, most frequently in the arm needed to operate the firing bolt of the soldier's rifle. The frequency of contractive paralysis brought on by hysteria was relatively high, and French military physicians in World War I invented the technique of *torporlage*—administering an electric current to the paralyzed limb—to treat it. A similar technique for treating the same condition was used by German and Russian military physicians. Once the soldier was removed from danger and given food and a few days' rest, the paralysis cured itself in most instances. This is exactly what appears to have happened to the French officer in 1807, since it was he who recorded the events described in his diary.

Suicide is yet another reaction sometimes provoked by the stress of war and it too appears quite often in military records of earlier battles. As the remnants of the French Grand Army fought their way out of Russia in 1812, an incident was recorded that had all the characteristics of a case of suicide resulting from emotional reaction to the stress of battle. A French officer in charge of an infantry battalion was hit in the thigh by a Russian cannonball that had ricocheted off the defensive palisade and broke his leg. An eyewitness recorded in his diary that the officer "fell, and without the least hesitation, finding that his wound was mortal, he coolly drew his pistols and blew out his brains before his troops. Terrified at this act of despair, his soldiers were completely scared. All of them at once threw down their arms and fled in disorder."[27]

Most combat officers are well aware that soldiers can be provoked to suicide either by the loneliness of military life or by the fear and stress of battle. In the American Army suicide usually occurs among new recruits who have difficulty adjusting to the separation from home which military life necessarily imposes. In the Soviet Army the rigor of military life seems to have made suicide a major problem. In a recent study based on interviews with Soviet troops, 49.6 percent of the soldiers said that "while they were in the military someone in their unit committed suicide," 53.1 percent reported that someone in their unit had attempted to commit suicide, and 84.1 percent reported that they had "heard stories about people committing suicide in other units."[28]

Among soldiers stationed in the American West in the 1860s suicide was almost epidemic. In 1867, the suicide rate among U.S. Army recruits posted to the western frontier was almost 6 percent, three times higher than the rate for British Army recruits stationed in similar circumstances.[29] Six of every hundred new recruits could be expected to destroy themselves by their own hand before their tour of duty was over! Suicide under fire, especially when things look desperate, occurs with a startling frequency. It happened among Custer's men at the battle of the Little Bighorn. In one well-documented case a group of Indians chased a soldier fleeing on horseback for nearly six miles. At the end of the chase the frightened soldier glanced back at the one remaining Indian warrior still giving chase, drew his pistol, and shot himself in the head.[30] In an even more macabre incident, Indian warriors who took part in the attack against Custer told journalists that as they began to overrun a group of soldiers who had taken cover behind their dead horses on a hillock, the soldiers began to shoot themselves and even each other! The Indians were so amazed at this self-destructive behavior that they broke off the attack and simply watched as the men killed themselves.[31]

During the Civil War there were no psychiatrists posted to the battlefront. (Such a development would not come until 1905, when the Russians were the first to do it.) However, military physicians were present and diagnosed cases of functional disability due to the fear of battle and the stress of military life. These physicians diagnosed a range of illnesses which are now known to be caused by emotional turbulence. These included "exhausted hearts," paralysis, severe palpitations (called "soldier's heart" at the time), war tremors, self-inflicted wounds, and nostalgia.[32] The only treatment for these disorders which seemed to work was relief from the line, rest, and, at times, a furlough for the soldier. Interestingly, soldiers on normal leave often collapsed with emotional illness at home even when they had shown no symptoms of mental debilitation before they left the fighting. Similar incidents were found among Israeli soldiers who had returned home for a brief respite from the 1983 Israeli-PLO war in Lebanon. In a great many cases, the brief "rest cure" prescribed by Civil War doctors resulted in the abatement of symptoms.

Union Army doctors diagnosed some severe conditions as "insanity"—a condition today termed psychosis—and insanity accounted for 6 percent of the medical discharges granted by the Union Army.[33] These physicians also dealt with a number of cases which they diagnosed as "feigned insanity," a condition in which emotional turbulence produced severe physiological symptoms but for which a physiological cause could not be found. These conditions included lameness, blindness, deafness, and lower back pain.[34] Today, psychiatrists diagnose such illnesses as conversion reactions. Emotional stress builds up in the soldier and, if no permissible emotional outlet is allowed, the soldier will "convert" his symptoms into physiological conditions. In World War II, Soviet military psychiatrists refused to accept debilitations resulting from purely emotional states, enforcing instead a strict rule that relief from battle was to be granted only to soldiers who had clearly defined physiological debilitations. As a consequence, Soviet soldiers "converted" their emotional stress into "legitimate" physical ailments in order to gain relief from the stress of war. It seems clear that the Soviet Army suffered disproportionately higher rates of conversion reactions in World War II than any other combat army.[35]

Even in peacetime minor conversion symptoms appear among troops under or about to endure stress. Medical doctors assigned to paratroop units, for example, routinely have to deal with psychosomatically induced complaints of lower back pain, even in experienced paratroopers, whenever the unit is scheduled to make a practice jump.

Fear and psychiatric debilitation are constant companions in any war. Engaging in battle is one of the most threatening, stressful, and horrifying experiences that man is expected to endure. Moreover, even in relatively small engagements, large numbers of men are usually involved. Accordingly, it is very likely that in any given battle combat reactions will be repeated many times over even if they do not come to the attention of military doctors. Severe emotional response to battle is neither a rare nor an isolated event. Indeed, it is becoming so common that the ability of armies to sustain their manpower levels in future wars is being brought into serious question. Modern war may simply have become too stressful for the soldier to tolerate for very long.

A Case Study in Combat Psychiatry

In examining those battles for which adequate eyewitness accounts are available, the researcher commonly finds that within a single battle, even small ones, the full range of psychiatric responses to stress emerge clearly. An excellent example is the battle of the Little Bighorn, in which George Armstrong Custer met his fate at the hands of thousands of Sioux and Cheyenne warriors.

As Custer was riding to his death against the main body of the Sioux, a unit of about three hundred men under the command of Major Marcus Reno was to act as a blocking force for the Custer attack. As things turned out, Reno's unit was trapped and forced to withdraw to a small bluff where he and his men fought a running defensive battle with the Indian enemy lasting two days and one night. In this engagement Reno's men suffered almost every major symptom of combat reaction now known to military psychiatry. Reno himself became a psychiatric casualty when he succumbed to acute battle shock syndrome.

In the midst of the battle Reno called his Indian scout, Yellow Knife, to his position amid a clump of sagebrush. As bullets and arrows whistled overhead, Reno drew very near Yellow Knife, probably to yell instructions in his ear. At this very instant Yellow Knife was struck square in the face by a bullet which sent his blood, flesh, and brains spattering all over Reno. Reno immediately went into shock. He began to foam at the mouth and his eyes rolled wildly in his head.[36] He was incapable of continuing in command or uttering any sounds that made sense. How long he remained in this condition is uncertain, but the diaries of men who were there report that he may have been out of action for at least a day.

Some of Reno's men were hysterically paralyzed with fear and were unable to function even to defend themselves. A small group of soldiers offered no resistance and the Indians considered them cowards and refused to kill them. Instead, they left Reno's men to the young boys, who dragged the soldiers away from each other and killed them without any resistance. In one case, a soldier was so terrified that the Indians refused to kill him, being content to strike him with pony whips. While this was going on Major Myles Moylan broke down completely and was unable to continue in command. The cavalry rescue force found him "blubbering like a whipped urchin, tears coursing down his cheeks."[37]

A very common reaction to the stress of battle is uncontrollable shaking, which can become so severe that men cannot fire their weapons. This condition is referred to as "war tremors." A number of soldiers recorded in their diaries that some of Reno's men suffered from such uncontrollable shaking that they could neither aim nor fire their weapons. In one case a soldier began shaking so violently that he eventually went into convulsions. His comrades had to bind him hand and foot to prevent him from injuring himself. In yet another instance a soldier suffered such fear that he lay in his rifle pit "crying like a child," unable to contribute to the fighting. In one of the most macabre instances of paralyzing fear, one soldier simply sat on the ground rubbing his head with both hands in abject confusion. Three Indians ran up to him, stretched him full length on his back, and decapitated him.[38] The poor soldier was unable to offer any resistance to his fate.

Soldiers' fears often increase at night when their senses play tricks on them. In Reno's command, some men began to hallucinate. One soldier records: "Private James Pym believed he saw renegade whites circling the rifle pits and shouting insults, challenging the troopers to come out. He thought these renegades carried the little swallowtail flags called guidons, and when Reno's bugler blew calls they would be exactly repeated. Other men saw columns of soldiers approaching and distinctly heard the calls of officers. Guns were fired to guide these rescuers and a trumpeter blew Stable Call."[39] Any soldier who has ever experienced night combat is well aware of the things one "sees" in the shadows. So many of Reno's men "saw" the same thing that there is little doubt that they were suffering combat reactions due to emotional tumult.

One soldier was suffering from acute neurasthenia and was lying face down on the ground. He was so still that the other soldiers thought for quite a while that he was dead. Two other soldiers maneuvering nearby came upon him, saw that he was alive, and told him to move. Although the soldier was conscious and looked right at them, he did not move. One of the soldiers kicked him, and he struggled to his feet, insisting that he was sick. Then "the man looked frightened to death. He walked a few steps and fell to the ground heedless of the heat of the sun or anything else going on around him."[40] Russian doctors in 1905 and again in World War I encountered the same condition many times. The soldiers had entered an asthenic fugue state approaching stupor caused by emotional exhaustion generated by fear.

During the two-day siege of Reno's command some soldiers pretended to be ill or wounded in order to get out of the fighting. As a practical matter, this was pointless since the medical station was in the middle of the battle area and offered neither cover nor concealment from enemy fire. One soldier, Private Billy Blake, pretended to be hurt and another claimed to be wounded and reported to the medical station. A quick examination showed only a slight burn on the abdomen. The other wounded men laughed at him and he was thrown out of the tent.[41] Soviet military doctors were acutely aware of this tendency of soldiers under stress to develop physical complaints and to use them to gain relief from battle. In World War II, it was common Soviet medical practice to keep medical facilities at a distance from the troops to make it difficult for them to report with minor complaints. Even today Soviet doctors are instructed that they should not get too near the troops for fear that they will iatrogenically "cause" these complaints by providing ready access to medical relief.

About the only thing that did not happen to Reno's men in the short two-day battle was desertion, surely because there was no place to go. But desertion, which is now commonly recognized as a secondary reaction to emotional stress, distinct from the flight or panic response, was endemic among soldiers on the American frontier. Between October 1866 and October 1867, more than 500 soldiers deserted from Custer's Seventh Cavalry alone. The desertion rate for the Seventh Cavalry reached 52 percent![42] Despite severe punishments, flogging, jail, branding, and tattooing—to say nothing of the difficulty of reaching civilization once outside the gates of the army post—in 1867 no less than 25 percent of the entire American frontier army deserted. Military discipline, though harsh, was also ineffective in stopping antisocial behavior among soldiers. In 1867 there were 13,000 recorded courts-martial in a single year, or about one for every two men in the frontier army.[43]

Conclusion

Men have known fear for at least as long as they have known war. The often stated belief that men in the past were more willing to accept their own deaths in the service of one thing or another is little more than an act of faith for which there is precious little objective support. It also seems true that men have always had difficulty dealing with the nearness of death as it emerges full-face in battle. In a great many instances fear has reached such proportions that it has quite literally driven soldiers mad and debilitated them to the point where they could no longer go on. Moreover, as the example of Reno's men at the Little Bighorn suggests, in any given battle men at war have manifested the full range of psychiatric reactions to fear. It is only the historical naïveté of modern men, who often seem ignorant of past human experiences, which leads them to conclude that only they have known fear in war. Perhaps we need such myths to sustain the belief that somehow we are different from those who have gone before. If so, a lot of historical reality must be ignored if the myth is to be maintained.

On the other hand, the fact that psychiatric casualties have appeared so often throughout the ages should not come as a surprise. Man has changed little physically or psychologically in the five thousand years of recorded history. The awareness of madness in one form or another is well documented in ancient texts. Psychiatry as a way of dealing with madness has been with us in one form or another since very ancient times. What is perhaps most interesting is that the psychiatric reactions to the fear of death and maiming have been remarkably consistent. One would have thought that the diversity of cultural conditioning in countless and vastly different societies would have affected the range of symptoms. It is clear, for example, from studies of psychiatric casualties in World War I that soldiers did in fact tend to manifest those psychiatric symptoms which had been defined by military medical authorities as "legitimate." In the case of Russian soldiers, the military psychiatry of the day defined "legitimate" psychiatric symptoms in purely physical terms. A soldier would not be allowed out of the fight until he had suffered some physical damage. If emotional causes were suspected, the Russians insisted that no soldier be relieved unless the emotional problem could be traced to some damaged physiology of the brain or central nervous system. As a result, Russian psychiatric casualties tended to manifest their emotional stress in precisely physical terms—paralysis, blindness, surdomutism, etc.—at rates far greater than found in other armies.

While it is accurate to say that in any battle a range of psychiatric symptoms will appear, it is impossible to reconstruct the rates at which such symptoms appeared in the past. No one began keeping records on psychiatric casualties with any degree of precision until the Russo-Japanese War of 1904–5. Moreover, military psychiatry was not considered a legitimate field of study until World War I. Psychiatry in general remained under the strong influence of neurology—

an approach which attributed aberrant behavior to damaged physiology—until World War II, when Freudian approaches to the explanation of emotional problems were first taken seriously by the American Army. In the past, because of ignorance of trauma-producing events, genuine psychiatric problems tended to be regarded as cowardice or lack of character. In one instance, for example, a soldier who tried to commit suicide by leaping from a house roof suffered a broken back. The attempt to kill himself was defined as cowardice and he was hanged, broken back and all.

It seems likely that the rates of psychiatric debilitation among combatants in the past must have been considerable, if not always obvious. We know today, for example, that many more men suffer severe emotional reactions than ever reach the medical stations, especially if their problems result in only partial debilitation. In World War II, studies of American soldiers engaged in combat revealed that more than three-quarters of them never fired their rifles at the enemy. Examples abound from the Civil War in which soldiers acted in a similar manner. In earlier battles, when masses of men fought each other, it was usually only the front rank that had to engage; those in the rear could safely do nothing. In engagements the size of Waterloo or Sedan, the opportunity for a soldier not to fire or to refuse to press the attack by merely falling down and remaining in the mud was too obvious for shaken men under fire to ignore. While there is no hard historical evidence to prove the point decisively, it nevertheless seems likely that armies of the past often lost at least some degree of combat power to the psychiatric reactions of emotionally disturbed soldiers.

It is important to understand the historical record of combat breakdown for the simple reason that while the technology of war has changed considerably over the centuries, the raw material of war—the men who must fight it—has changed little or not at all. This suggests that the technology of war, though important, is not the decisive factor in victory or defeat. As Xenophon made clear three thousand years ago, it is still the "soul" of the soldier that is most important. Technology, no matter how sophisticated or deadly, will mean nothing if men cannot withstand the storm of battle.

The leaders of modern armies, with their large staffs of technical experts, tend all too readily to forget this lesson and busy themselves with the details of "orchestrating" or "servicing" the battlefield through the employment of sophisticated technologies. They appear secure in the faith, historically quite unfounded, that soldiers can be made to do what the technology requires of them. Such military managers believe that today's soldier is somehow different from those who took the field in the past. What the lessons of the past ought to teach is that men in battle break down, technology notwithstanding. It is man, not his machines, that sets the ultimate limits on battle performance. At the same time, however, there is no doubt that the technology of war has become so destructive that it has raised the question of whether any soldier except the already insane can long endure the battlefields of the future. What evidence we have suggests that the limits of human endurance have already been reached.

3

War and the Limits of Human Endurance

Although men have suffered psychiatric breakdowns in war for centuries, it has not been a subject with which military establishments have been overly concerned. For much of military history, psychiatric breakdown in war has been conveniently dismissed as the isolated acts of cowards or the weak, a view which was generally held in the U.S. military up through World War II. Nor is it a subject with which the general public has been concerned or familiar. Most people who have not seen combat are conditioned by their perception of warfare in general, a view obtained mostly through the media and, in wartime, through a carefully controlled press. In World War I pictures and stories about troops at the front were carefully limited to reporting successes. Photographs were screened so that the civilian population would not be upset by too graphic a view of the realities of war.[1] While it is common for all governments to restrict information in wartime, Americans in particular, because of their

70

lack of actual experience with war, have received their view of war mostly through motion pictures and television shows, a view that is all too often unrealistic and romantic.

However war is portrayed for mass audiences, soldiers breaking down under the strain of battle are rarely, if ever, portrayed. In those few instances which do show a soldier in collapse, the condition is portrayed as rare and lasting only a minute or so, after which the soldier is brought around by a slap or some other minor treatment by an officer, sergeant, or comrade, usually complete with a lecture on military duty. Because Americans have been so ignorant of the realities of war, they remain largely ignorant of the true nature of psychiatric casualties. The prevailing view is that soldiers who break under the strain of battle are weak or cowardly.

This simplistic view is, unfortunately, often shared by military men as well. To be sure, there has, beginning with World War I, always been a small core of medical officers who have tried desperately to get the attention of their superiors in order to force them to take the problem more seriously. While they met with some success in World War I, the lessons which they learned were almost completely lost by the time World War II broke out. The result was a medical disaster in dealing with psychiatric casualties in World War II. It was only near the end of the war that medical facilities for dealing with the problem were put into place and made to work reasonably well. The performance of military psychiatric facilities in the Vietnam War left much to be desired.

The belief that psychiatric casualties occur only among men who are cowards or innately weak, whose character flaws and personality weaknesses dispose them to breaking down in battle, has led the military for most of this century to adopt a model of psychiatric breakdown which is grossly incorrect. That model was based on the assumption that some men were more predisposed by their nature to breakdown. Thus, the model used by the U.S. military was: predisposition + stress = psychiatric collapse.[2] This model was used for the first time in World War I, when, after numerous complaints from commanders at the front about the mental quality and durability of their troops, military authorities instituted a more vigorous screening of recruits. Although the approach seemed logical, it didn't work very well when used during the last months of World War I. Despite this experience, during the interwar period (1918–41) most military psychiatrists continued to believe that if too many soldiers were suffering mental collapse, then the answer was to select from the general populace only the strong who could be expected to endure the stress of war.

World War II saw the first large-scale systematic use of recruit screening for psychiatric disposition to mental collapse. In World War II the U.S. military examined 18,000,000 men for military service. Of these, 5,250,000 were rejected (29 percent) as unfit for combat for physical reasons. The military rejected an additional 970,000 men for neuropsychiatric disorders and emotional problems. Thus, psychiatric exemptions accounted for 18.5 percent of the total rejections, a rate that was twenty times greater than that of the Soviet Army, which employed no psychiatric screening.[3] The American soldiers who went to war, then, had been screened for potential psychiatric disposition to breakdown and the "weak" were presumed to have been eliminated.

The results of this screening were disappointing. The rejection rate for recruits for World War II was almost seven times higher than for World War I. Yet, despite the attempt to eliminate the "weak" from the military manpower pool, psychiatric casualties were admitted to military hospitals at twice the World War I rate and separations for mental and emotional reasons showed a nearly sevenfold increase over the World War I rate! In fact, psychiatric casualties were the largest single category of military disabilities granted by the government in World War II.[4] Whatever the psychiatric screening of conscripts accomplished, it had certainly not reduced the rate of psychiatric casualties on the battlefield.

The view that only the "weak" collapse under the strain of war or that psychiatric collapse in battle is rare can only be maintained if one is prepared to ignore a great deal of evidence. Closer to the truth is the view that psychiatric breakdown in war is all too common; that given enough stress and exposure to battle, almost all soldiers will suffer some degree of psychiatric debilitation. Psychiatric breakdown has nothing to do with being "weak" or cowardly. It is an inevitable result of the nature of war.

If one examines the extent of psychiatric collapse in America's wars in this century, no other conclusion is possible. During World War I, almost 2,000,000 men were sent overseas to fight in Europe. Of these, 116,516 met death in battle. Another 204,002 were wounded.[5] There were, however, 106,000 soldiers admitted to military medical facilities for psychiatric reasons, 69,394 of whom were so mentally shaken that they were evacuated and permanently lost to the fighting effort.[6] Some 36,600 represented a long-term loss to the fighting ability of the American Army, being hospitalized for periods lasting from several weeks to several months.[7] Many of those who were returned to the fighting broke down again. Approximately 53,000 additional soldiers, those who reported to medical facilities suffering from psychiatric problems but who were returned to the front almost immediately—that is, within a few days—were lost to the battle for a short period of time. The point is, however, that they suffered some degree of psychiatric debilitation. Again, many of these suffered relapses after they returned to the front. The data indicate that 158,994 soldiers were out of action for some period of time for purely psychiatric reasons.

If the evidence from World War I was insufficient to convince those still in doubt about the frequency and inevitability of psychiatric breakdown, the experience gained in World War II should certainly have been more convincing. Over one million men—1,393,000—suffered psychiatric symptoms serious enough to debilitate them for some period. In the U.S. Army ground forces alone (not counting

Army air crews, Marines, and Navy), 504,000 men were permanently lost to the fighting effort for psychiatric reasons—enough manpower to outfit fifty combat divisions![8] Of these, 330,000 men were lost to ground combat units in the European theater and received separations for psychiatric reasons. Another 596,000 were lost to the fighting effort for periods of weeks or months and eventually returned to the line, and still another 464,500 reported to medical facilities for treatment without being admitted and were returned to the line almost immediately.[9]

Once again these figures understate the magnitude of the problem. In World War II the ratio of rear-area support troops to actual combatants was about twelve to one. In four years of war, no more than about 800,000 U.S. ground soldiers saw direct combat. Of these, 37.5 percent became such serious psychiatric cases that they were lost to the military effort for the duration of the war and given discharges. Another 596,000, or about 74 percent, were admitted to medical facilities for psychiatric problems for a length of time ranging from weeks to months. Many were eventually returned to the combat effort. Although some casualties needed repeated treatment and thus reported or were admitted more than once, the fact is that, in a statistical sense, every American soldier in the European theater was at risk of becoming a psychiatric casualty! It was not only the "weak" or the cowardly that were cracking under the strain of war.

It should be clear that while the strain of battle does not cause everyone to become a psychiatric casualty and not all men succumb as rapidly as others, combat does functionally debilitate very great numbers of men who, although they don't collapse and require treatment, are still functionally debilitated to the point where they cannot contribute to the fighting effort. The degree of functional debilitation is really much greater than the actual rate of psychiatric casualties would indicate. In World War II, interviews were conducted with men in over four hundred line companies who saw direct combat in both the European and Pacific theaters. All the soldiers had been in close combat. The results of that study indicate that in any given combat engagement no more than 15 percent of the soldiers ever fired their weapons at the enemy even if they were being attacked![10] Even in elite companies with veteran soldiers and a reputation for aggressiveness, the number rarely rose to 25 percent.[11] The same findings emerged from a study of Air Force fighter pilots. Less than 1 percent of these pilots accounted for over 40 percent of enemy kills.[12] Most pilots never shot anyone down or ever tried to. The reason for this unwillingness is fear. Fully 75 percent of experienced combat soldiers in World War II were too frightened to fire their weapons during an attack or even to defend themselves against an enemy attack. That all these men were cowards or "weak" hardly seems credible.

The Korean War produced fewer psychiatric casualties than either World War I or World War II. Initially the rates of psychiatric debilitation were greater than the rates in both world wars; in the early days of the war, as the front collapsed, there were few medical facilities to deal with the problem. In the first year of the war, the rate of psychiatric casualties was 250 per 1,000 men, or almost seven times higher than the average rate for World War II! As the war settled down, the lines stabilized, and medical psychiatric teams were dispatched to the battle zone, psychiatric casualties dropped to 70 per 1,000 in 1951, to 22 per 1,000 in 1952, and down to 21 per 1,000 in the first six months of 1953. The average rate, at 32 per 1,000 was slightly lower than that of World War II.[13]

Once again, however, the raw data paint an even more dismal picture of psychiatric collapse in battle. Of the 1,587,040 men who served in Korea, 33,629 were killed by hostile fire and another 103,284 wounded.[14] The number of psychiatric casualties admitted to military medical facilities for treatment was 48,002, a number greater than the total number of men killed in the war. The chances of becoming a psychiatric casualty were 143 percent greater than being killed. But of the 1,587,040 soldiers who served in Korea, only 198,380 saw actual combat. While only 17 percent of these combatants were killed, 24.2 percent became psychiatric casualties serious enough to require treatment for some period of time. The combatant in Korea was one and a half times as likely to become a psychiatric casualty as to be killed by enemy fire.

The Vietnam War was, by normal standards of combat intensity, not much of a war. It was a war in which the degree of actual battle contact was low, and when contact did occur, it was relatively brief and not very intense. The number of psychiatric casualties during that ten-year war was relatively low at the beginning, increased to higher rates during the fierce fighting of the Tet offensive of 1968, and then, paradoxically, as the intensity of battle fell off in 1970–71, the number of psychiatric casualties rose even higher. Most of these later casualties were due to nostalgia, what the U.S. military termed "disorders of loneliness." Early in the war, evacuations for psychiatric reasons reached only 6 percent of total medical evacuations out of the combat zone. By 1971, this rate had increased to almost 50 percent.[15]

Of the 2.8 million men who saw service in Vietnam only a small proportion, about 280,000 men over a ten-year period, were actually engaged in direct combat. The average psychiatric casualty rate was 12 per 1,000 men of the total force, or 35,200 soldiers admitted to military medical facilities for psychiatric reasons. The war's lack of intensity can be seen in the fact that of the 2.8 million men deployed in-country, 45,735 men were killed by enemy action, or about only 1.6 percent of the total force. However, when compared to the number of men who actually saw combat, the number of dead amount to 16 percent of the combat force and the number of psychiatric casualties reached 12.6 percent of the same force.

For reasons that will be addressed later, the Vietnam War was unique in America's military history and those qualities which made it unique also worked to reduce battle intensity and thus the number of psychiatric casualties. It was these same circumstances, however, that produced another unique result: the number of soldiers who suffered psychiatric symptoms and debilitation after the war was over and they were safely home. There are no precise data on the number of soldiers who suffered from Post-Traumatic Stress Disorder after the Vietnam War. Figures range from 500,000 to 1,500,000 PTSD cases, figures which indicate that at least 18 percent and possibly as much as 54 percent of the force suffered psychiatric symptoms.[16] While there is disagreement on the exact numbers of such victims, there is widespread agreement that the Vietnam War produced more victims of PTSD, in both relative and absolute numbers, than any other war in American history. While the chances that a soldier would become a psychiatric casualty in Vietnam were about the same as being killed in action, there is no doubt that the chances that he would eventually suffer delayed psychiatric symptoms as a direct consequence of his experiences were much greater than in any of the previous wars.

In every war in which American soldiers have fought in this century, the chances of becoming a psychiatric casualty—of being debilitated for some period of time as a consequence of the stresses of military life—were greater than the chances of being killed by enemy fire. The only exception was the Vietnam War, in which the chances were almost equal. If one includes those who suffered Post-Traumatic Stress Disorder, then once again more soldiers suffered psychiatric collapse than death from enemy fire. While it seems true, as we shall see, that there may exist a vulnerability to psychiatric breakdown peculiar to the American soldier, it is worth pointing out that 30 percent of the casualties suffered by the Israeli Defense Force in the 1973 Yom Kippur war were psychiatric. In the 1982 Lebanon invasion, not much of a war by any standard, the number of Israeli psychiatric casualties exceeded the number of dead by more than 150 percent.[17]

While the vulnerabilities of a particular people may cause

their soldiers to crack more readily under the strain of combat, psychiatric collapse is due far more to the nature of modern warfare itself. In a war, even a war that is fairly low in intensity, the strain on the human psyche is often too much to bear. It is war, not man, that is at fault. He has created a horror with which he cannot deal in a rational manner and it threatens to destroy him. As a U.S. Army medical report written in World War II notes, "the key to an understanding of the psychiatric problem is the simple fact that the danger of being killed or maimed imposes a strain so great that it causes men to break down. One look at the shrunken, apathetic faces of psychiatric cases as they come stumbling into the medical station, sobbing, trembling, referring shudderingly to 'them shells' and to buddies mutilated or dead, is enough to convince most observers of this fact. There is no such thing as 'getting used to combat.' Each man 'up there' knew that at any moment he might be killed, a fact kept constantly before his mind by the sight of the dead and mutilated buddies around him. Each moment of combat imposes a strain so great that men will break down in direct relation to the intensity and duration of their exposure. Thus, psychiatric casualties are as inevitable as gunshot and shrapnel wounds in warfare . . ."[18]

There is, then, no evidence to support the commonly held view among the civilian populace, fostered by movies and television programs, that only the weak or the cowardly break down in battle. In reality, everyone is susceptible to psychiatric breakdown in war. Perhaps most telling, not only are there no personality or demographic factors which are associated with psychiatric collapse in war; neither are there any factors associated with heroism. It is impossible to predict which soldiers will collapse and which will behave bravely.[19] All men seem equally at risk to become either heroes or psychiatric basket cases, and there is no way to predict which will become which. Worse still, a soldier who performs admirably one day may, quite unexpectedly, become a psychiatric casualty the next. When men are exposed to enough combat, there is no statistical difference in the rates of psychiatric breakdown among inexperienced troops and battle-hardened veterans. All are at risk in war.[20]

Where all men are equally at risk to be broken by the horror of battle, it seems ludicrous to talk of norms in war. When so many men, quite normal in every other way, succumb to psychiatric pressures and can no longer function, in what sense can such men be said to deviate from the norm of expected behavior? In what sense, if any, can breakdown in battle be considered abnormal? The rates at which soldiers become debilitated suggest quite strongly that psychiatric breakdown is precisely what normal men do when the strain becomes too great. It is the reaction of a sane man to want to escape the horror of war, and mental collapse is simply the means he chooses to escape.

There is enough evidence from studies done after World War II to suggest that the only people who do not succumb to the stress of war are those who are already mentally aberrant in a clinically defined sense. About 2 percent of soldiers exposed to combat over long periods of time do not break under the stress. An examination of these "heroes" reveals that their most commonly held trait was that they were "aggressive psychopathic personalities" who were this way before they entered the battle zone.[21] The lesson seems to be that only the sane break down. Those already mentally ill appear able to adjust to the horror of combat. Perhaps it is simply that while collective insanity can destroy normally sane men, it cannot reverse individual insanity.

The Dynamics of Mental Collapse

In a physiological sense man is as much biological animal as any other animal. He is equipped with the normal physiological mechanisms of any animal which prepare the body to deal with and survive under stress. As in other animals, the normal accompaniment of emotion is muscular action as the autonomic system and endocrine glands bring the body to a heightened state of physical excitement to cope with danger. Man's inborn instincts are the same as any other animal: to recognize danger and to deal with it by "flight or fight."

Under severe stress the body automatically goes into action. The soldier's blood pressure rises, his heart beats rapidly, he begins to sweat, his muscles tense, his short-term muscular strength increases, his mind races, and the endocrine system activates all the biological mechanisms which contribute to increased sensory awareness and muscular power. Few soldiers have any real control of these physiological reactions to stress. Once the danger is gone, the body will gradually calm down as the biological systems which produced the stress response return to their normal state.

But what happens when the stressful situation—the perception of danger of death and mutilation on the battlefield—is of long duration? In these circumstances the body will maintain itself in a high state of readiness since the presence of danger automatically sustains the physiological responses needed to deal with it. Unfortunately, no one can endure at this level of biological tension for very long without becoming physically exhausted. Moreover, if the danger produces a stress response long enough—days, for example—the body's biological systems which sustain the physiology of stress will become fixated to the point where only prolonged rest away from danger will enable the body to reduce its state of readiness. A soldier in this state will eventually collapse from nervous exhaustion—the body simply will burn out.

But if man is part animal, he also has an intellect, the faculty which allows him to make reasoned judgments about circumstances he must confront and to make choices about his actions. That is why it makes no sense to attribute such qualities as heroism or cowardice to animals; they react in the only way they can react, guided almost entirely by biological reactions and instinct. Because man can choose, it is only he who passes judgment on the choices of his fellows and decides whether they have acted bravely or not. And because he can choose, his mind can permit him to choose actions that overrule or contradict the impulses of his physiology.

A soldier's body, exhausted by his physiological reactions to stress, will affect the way his mind functions. One of the first faculties to degenerate under stress is the ability to process information and make decisions. Moreover, a physically fatigued body will surely collapse regardless of the amount of willpower exhibited by the soldier. The old military maxim of basic training that "your body will do it if your mind makes you do it" is, for the most part, untrue. Conversely, the psyche can affect the physiological operations of the body in any number of ways. Psychosomatic illnesses, conditions of genuine physical debilitation, are brought on by affective mental states in which the mind is able to produce physical ailments and, in some cases, even cause the physical deterioration of body organs. One of the most interesting of these illnesses is nostalgia, mentioned earlier. In the Civil War, soldiers suffering from nostalgia quite often died from physical ailments which their mental states created. Civil War autopsies of soldiers suffering from "exhausted hearts" discovered clear evidence of physiological deterioration of the blood vessels when there was no other medical reason for them to deteriorate. Today, stomach ulcers and colitis and other diseases are commonly recognized as being brought on by continued stress. The mind and body coexist and either may readily affect the ability of the other to function properly, especially under conditions of great stress.

But the mind is not defenseless and, fortunately, it is not autonomic in its reactions to stress. What men believe and think can have a great bearing on how they behave when confronted with danger. In this regard, Jules Masserman suggests that all human psychic defense rests on three key beliefs—"the Ur defenses of man"—which serve to shore up the psyche against danger.[22] The first of these beliefs is that there is a connection between a man's actions and what happens to him. Man simply cannot live in a purely random world (as battle often appears to be). He must believe that there is some connection between what he does and what eventually happens to him, especially in times of danger. Otherwise he will go insane.

The second belief needed to sustain the psyche in a state of contact with reality is the faith that "someone will help me." Man is sustained by the belief (however unfounded at times) that he is not alone and that if he does all he can to survive and the danger still grows, someone—perhaps even God—will come to his aid and save him. It is precisely this belief that leads some men under great stress to develop a physically debilitating illness. By becoming incapacitated, a condition which clearly does not improve his chances for survival, the individual retreats from reality and shifts responsibility for his survival to someone else who will keep him safe. Studies from World Wars I and II show that when prisoners of war were subjected to artillery attack or aerial bombardment, none of the prisoners—who had, by being captured, shifted responsibility for their survival to their guards—suffered psychiatric reactions, whereas their guards did. Men sustain their sanity with the belief that when all else fails, someone will come to their aid. This often accounts for extreme religiosity among soldiers in danger. When confronted with the suspicion that this belief may be false, men invariably come apart.

The third belief that lies at the center of man's psychic survival is the conviction that "I will live forever." Even under the most trying of circumstances, men must continue to believe that they will somehow survive or else they collapse. The desire to survive is so deeply embedded in our genetic makeup as to be self-evident. When confronted with the face of death from which there is no escape, few men can retain their sanity.

Men build their lives and social institutions on these basic beliefs. Subcultures and social institutions like the military buttress these beliefs by inculcating corollary beliefs in the individual soldier. Thus, all soldiers are taught to be brave, to stand firm when battle begins, to keep faith with one's friends. The individual soldier comes to define himself in terms of these corollary beliefs so that to be a good soldier is to act according to them.

Soldiers in combat are constantly confronted with stark evidence that none of the basic assumptions upon which their mental stability is premised are valid. The evidence of the battlefield—the noise, the randomness of death, its constancy, the shattered bodies—shakes the individual's faith in his basic assumptions about life. He is left only with the corollaries developed by the military and even these become subject to severe doubt as the evidence mounts that they too offer no safety from the horror which surrounds him.

A soldier in combat develops a constant and severe conflict between his physiology's autonomic functions designed to keep him alive and the mental pull of his beliefs, already seriously eroded by the evidence of his senses. He wants to live up to the ideals of being a good soldier, but his fear pulls him in the other direction. To make matters worse, the soldier fears not only what is happening but also what can happen. This ability to project fear produces a constant state of anxiety which grows with each hour and each day. Thus, "the soldier is suffering from a conflict between his fear of death and injury and his own ideals of duty. . . . With anxiety, however, since the fear element is directed to what *might* happen and not to what *is* happening, there is nothing that can be done and the autonomic system runs riot . . . the commonest process by which relief is obtained is by the conversion of the anxiety state into a hysterical symptom. . . . Paralysis, blindness, deafness or indeed any illness gives him an honorable retreat from the situation, and his conflict is solved and his anxiety relieved."[23]

While the dynamics of mental collapse are clear enough, the onset of a soldier's breakdown can be rapid or gradual.

A soldier debilitated by psychiatric breakdown is usually said to be suffering from battle shock. Battle shock can be clinically described as acute (often called combat shock) or gradual (often called combat fatigue) depending upon the speed with which symptoms manifest themselves. In general, about 50 percent of all psychiatric casualties suffer acute onset of symptoms, usually within five days of being exposed to battle, while another 50 percent develop them "gradually," usually within thirty days of exposure to combat.[24] In specific instances, of course, the distribution can vary. In the Israeli invasion of Lebanon in 1982, 100 percent of the Israeli psychiatric cases were battle shock cases developed in six days of war or less.

Gradual combat shock (combat fatigue) develops in four stages. At any stage, however, the soldier's ability to function efficiently as a combat soldier is diminished to some degree. Almost from the moment of exposure to combat the soldier's effectiveness diminishes and almost immediately his mental state is characterized by anxiety. During the first few days of combat most men enter a state of fluctuating fear. The symptoms of fear make themselves manifest in a number of ways, including increased frequency and urgency of urination, intense thirst, a refusal to eat which often leads to anorexia, in which food cannot be consumed or, if it is, it is vomited. There is an increasing fear of being alone or of being exposed to enemy fire even for a few seconds. Men will often defecate in their pants rather than leave the cover of their positions to relieve themselves. The old Army adage about using one's helmet for a toilet has some basis in actual practice.

During various periods of tension, such as incoming artillery from harassing fire, soldiers manifest great increases in sweating, vasomotor instability, and other overt physiological signs of fear. Almost all soldiers develop muscular tremors to some degree and many shake so uncontrollably that they cannot perform even the most rudimentary tasks, such as loading their weapons. Although soldiers in the unit may have trained together, deployed together, and many may have become friends, there is a growing tendency not to share articles such as blankets, shelter, food, or ammunition.[25] This first stage of combat fatigue usually lasts about five to seven days, and during this period a significant number of men will succumb to acute combat shock and have to be evacuated.

Those who do not break down now enter a period where their confidence in themselves, their weapons, their comrades, and their own fighting ability increases. They are able to distinguish the sounds of enemy weapons from those of friendly forces, are able to react as trained in fire discipline and night concealment, watch for snipers, and otherwise perform as "battle-wise" soldiers are expected to perform. In the first stage their physiological reactions had become so intense that they interfered with their ability to function. In this second stage these biological reactions, although more elevated than those found among men in the civilian population, are at least reduced to a level where they no longer interfere with the soldier's ability to perform adequately.[26] It is during this period that the soldier reaches his maximum fighting capability. On average, the period lasts about fourteen days. After this, the soldier begins to manifest symptoms of combat fatigue to an even greater degree.

After three weeks on the line more serious symptoms of combat exhaustion begin to appear. The soldier easily becomes physically exhausted after only minor periods of exertion; he is always tired and no amount of sleep or rest on the line will relieve the condition. Fatigue is no longer being caused by the soldier's physiology, but is being psychologically generated. The whole set of fear reactions that were evident in stage one reappear with increased intensity, and his ability to suppress them is less successful. The soldier again loses his military skills and is once again unable to distinguish friendly from enemy fire, outgoing artillery from incoming fire, and he becomes overcautious. He often will not come out from his position for any reason. He is unable to sleep, and the more exhausted he becomes, the more unable he is to get sleep or rest of any kind. When he does sleep, it is usually during the day, because of the greater feeling of insecurity he feels at night. Irritability increases and a number of soldiers manifest severe emotional outbursts of anger over minor matters. Tremors become constant and often the soldier rushes around ceaselessly changing his position to reduce the chances of being hit by enemy fire.[27] This period lasts about a week or so.

After being on the line for five weeks, the soldier enters the fourth phase of combat fatigue. The loss of friends who have been killed or wounded and the mounting casualty toll engender in him a feeling of helplessness and hopelessness. He begins to believe that he will be either killed or wounded and that he cannot go on. The soldier's mental processes begin to deteriorate and he becomes apathetic and unable to comprehend simple orders or directions. His memory begins to fail him to such an extent that he can no longer be relied upon to remember simple instructions. His battle skills are manifestly absent and he no longer remembers how to react to even minor situations. The soldier cannot concentrate on anything except thoughts of home and the constant thought of death in which the anxiety that he might be killed is replaced by the certainty that he will be. Tremors disappear and even the most threatening combat actions cannot raise him from his general state of lassitude and listlessness.[28]

If the soldier is not evacuated at this point—about five to six weeks after his initial exposure to combat—he will likely enter a vegetative state where he is incapable of any action at all. Such states can and do approach catatonia. Very often, however, a soldier in this state will suddenly collapse under the impact of a specific incident, such as a near-miss or the death of a close friend. While the reactions to such events vary, all too often soldiers undergo a violent, sudden emotional explosion and begin to run around wildly and aimlessly with total disregard for their safety. Some become amnesic and others become stuporous and unable to walk, see, or hear. Still others will panic and run into artillery fire or even at the enemy guns, while others find a trench or hole and refuse to come out, remaining there crying or trembling out of control. Some men will fall on the ground and claw at the earth screaming. At this point, of course, the soldier has suffered a shattering emotional collapse and must be evacuated.

The simple fact is that men are crushed by the strain of modern war. Judging from the data presented earlier, all men are at risk of becoming psychiatric casualties and, in fact, most men will collapse given enough exposure to battle stress. There is no such thing as getting used to combat. Nevertheless, studies of World War II soldiers revealed that about 2 percent do not collapse. But these men are already mad, for most of them were aggressive psychopathic personalities before they entered battle. It is only the sane who break down.

It is interesting to note that soldiers can break down in remarkable numbers at even the thought of being forced to go into battle. Of the 970,000 men whom the U.S. Army rejected for military service for emotional reasons in World War II, many were suffering fear reactions to the very prospect of being sent into the military. Many had no history of emotional problems prior to being drafted. Moreover, of the 504,000 men who were separated from military service for psychiatric reasons after they had been inducted and sent to training bases, a substantial number were separated in the United States even before they had either been deployed overseas or received orders to deploy.[29] In units that had been alerted for deployment to combat, psychiatric symptoms began to appear as much as eighty days before the unit actually shipped out.[30] And these symptoms were hardly minor. Once a unit was alerted for combat deployment, there was a great increase in the number of somatic complaints such as heart palpitations, dyspnea, general weakness, abdominal pain, vomiting, and backache. Many soldiers were hospitalized for these complaints and never returned to their units for deployment.[31] There were also large increases at this time in the number of self-inflicted wounds and accidents. The thought of going to war is sufficient to drive some men to develop psychiatric symptoms.

What must be kept in mind is that those soldiers who were sent into battle and eventually became psychiatric casualties were not a representative cross section of the American Army. Quite the contrary. They had been screened for psychiatric problems upon induction, screened again during Stateside training, again prior to deployment, again in their overseas training bases, and finally again before being sent into battle. The "weak" among them had already been removed or removed themselves by manifesting a range of psychiatric symptoms severe enough to functionally debilitate them. Those who finally went into battle were the strongest of the lot and many of them still succumbed to the stress of battle. War has simply become too stressful for even the strongest among us to stand for very long.

The Victims

To describe the dynamics of psychiatric breakdown in battle does little to describe the actual terrors that the psychiatric casualty lives with. The soldier suffering from combat shock often undergoes suffering that most civilians, save those incarcerated in mental institutions, cannot imagine. What battle often does is to take a reasonably normal and sane individual and, sometimes in a matter of hours, transform him into a victim whose pain far exceeds anything most civilians ever suffer or witness. Nations customarily measure the "costs of war" in dollars, lost production, or the number of soldiers killed or wounded. Rarely do military establishments attempt to measure the costs of war in terms of individual human suffering. Psychiatric breakdown remains one of the most costly items of war when expressed in human terms.

Since the end of World War I, military medical establishments have outlined the major psychiatric conditions which soldiers suffer in war, but it must be quickly added that the human mind seems infinite in its potential to produce widely different symptoms of battle shock. An examination of these categories of symptomologies reveals just how terrible the mental and physical condition of a battle-shocked soldier can be.

FATIGUE CASES: : A soldier suffering from "simple" fatigue is mentally and physically exhausted; his autonomic biological systems, after periods of hyperactivity in keeping his physiology at a heightened state in order to deal with danger, have collapsed. The physical exhaustion begins to erode his mental strength and he is aware that his mental powers are deteriorating. The fatigue state is clinically "prodromal"—that is, it sets the stage for further and more complete collapse. If the soldier is not treated or evacuated, further collapse is inevitable. In a state of fatigue the soldier finds physical motion difficult if not impossible. If they are available, he will tend to indulge excessively in alcohol, tobacco, or, as in the Vietnam War, light and heavy drugs. He will begin to manifest a tendency to become unsociable and overly irritable. Eventually, he will lose interest in all activities with his comrades and will seek to avoid any responsibility or activity involving effort. The soldier will be prone to emotional crises such as crying fits or fits of extreme anxiety or terror. There will also be accompanying somatic symptoms such as hypersensitivity to sound, increased sweating, palpitations, and cyanosis of the extremities.[32] If he is forced to remain in the battle zone, this state of fatigue will eventually develop into deeper psychiatric symptoms.

CONFUSIONAL STATES: : A soldier suffering from exhaustion can quickly shift into a confusional state, which is generally marked by a psychotic dissociation from reality. He no longer knows where he is. Unable to deal with his environment anymore, he mentally removes himself from it. Often such states involve delirium of some sort and are likely to eventually produce schizophrenic states of dissociation. Frequently, manic-depressive psychosis develops in which wild swings of mood and activity are evident. One often noted response is the development of Ganzer Syndrome. Confronted with the horror of war all around him, a soldier afflicted with Ganzer Syndrome will begin to make jokes, act silly, and otherwise try to ward off the horror with humor and the ridiculous. The degree of affliction in confusional states ranges from the profoundly neurotic to the overtly psychotic.[33]

CONVERSION HYSTERIA: : Conversion hysteria is one of the most pronounced and dramatic manifestations of battle shock. The soldier, torn between his fears and his socially derived notions of duty, "resolves" the extreme tension by "converting" his fears into some somatic symptom severe enough to incapacitate himself and thus gain relief from the terror he faces. The physical symptoms allow him to gain relief from the terror with a "legitimate" physical condition, thus preserving his self-respect in the eyes of himself and his peers.[34] After all, no one can rightly expect a soldier who has become blind or paralyzed to continue to fight.

Conversion hysteria can occur traumatically or in posttraumatic situations. Thus, a soldier can manifest hysteria after he has been knocked out by concussion, after receiving a minor nondebilitating wound, or after a near-miss. Hysteria can also manifest itself after a wounded soldier has been evacuated. Once he is in a hospital or safely in a rear area, hysteria begins to emerge, most often as a defense against returning to the fight.[35] Wherever it occurs, it is the mind which produces the physical symptoms of debilitation.

Conversion hysteria involves massive and partial dissociative states.[36] Massive dissociation manifests itself in fugue states—an inability to know where one is or to function at all—often accompanied by aimless wandering around the battlefield with complete disregard for evident dangers. Very often, a soldier in a fugue state is totally or partially amnesic, blocking out from his consciousness large parts of his past and present memory. The psychosis can also take the form of twilight states—repeated passing in and out of consciousness—sometimes accompanied by severe and uncontrollable tremors. Often, hysteria degenerates into convulsive attacks in which the soldier rolls into the fetal position and begins to shake violently, much as he would during an epileptic seizure. Finally, dissociation can manifest itself in complete catatonia or other states of physical rigidity in which it is impossible to move at all.

States of partial dissociation, while clinically less serious in principle, nonetheless produce horrible symptoms. Among the most common afflictions are hysterical paralysis, deafness, and blindness.[37] The mind literally forces the body to become incapacitated. In World Wars I and II, for example, cases of contractive paralysis of the arm were rather common. In this situation, the soldier's arm not only became paralyzed but often contracted in such a way that the hand became rigidly fixed to the shoulder. The psychosomatic nature of the condition was clearly evident; most often the arm which became paralyzed was the arm used to operate the firing bolt mechanism of the rifle. Thus, in left-handed men the paralysis occurred in the left arm, whereas in right-handed soldiers the right arm was affected. Sometimes the soldier suffered paralysis of one or both legs. The soldier is indeed paralyzed or deaf or, perhaps most terrifying, blind. Soldiers suffering from partial dissociative hysterical states also undergo acute sensory disturbances, including somatic pain. Often this manifests itself in the feeling that sections of the body are numb or the skin feels inflamed or in the appearance of "left infra-mammary pain" simulating the conditions of a heart attack.[38]

ANXIETY STATES: : Generalized anxiety in soldiers suffering from combat shock is characterized by a feeling of total weariness and tenseness that cannot be relieved by sleep or rest which degenerates into an inability to concentrate. The soldier, when he can sleep, is often awakened by terrible nightmares associated with battle experiences. Eventually, the soldier becomes fixated on the idea of death and interprets the events of the battlefield as being directed at him personally. He becomes obsessed with death and the fear that he will fail or that the other men in his unit will discover that he is frightened. If the anxiety state is allowed to persist without relief, the soldier will develop phobic conditions, an extreme fear focused on some object. Thus, he might refuse to go near a tank for fear that it will draw enemy fire that will kill him. Generalized anxiety can easily slip into hysteria.

Anxiety often makes itself manifest in a range of severe somatic neuroses, such as effort syndrome, an abnormal physiological reaction to effort. Frequently it is accompanied by shortness of breath, weakness, precordial pain, blurred vision, giddiness, vasomotor abnormalities, and fainting. Another reaction is emotional hypertension, in which the soldier's blood pressure rises dramatically with all the accompanying symptoms of weakness, sweating, nervousness, etc. He may develop severe palpitations (soldier's heart) along with it. A range of stress-related somatic problems frequently develop, including peptic ulcers, stress dyspepsia, backache, and emotional diarrhea.

OBSESSIONAL AND COMPULSIVE STATES: : These states of psychiatric breakdown are similar to those found in conversion hysteria except that in conversion states the soldier is often completely dissociated from his symptoms and is not aware that they are caused by his own fears and anxieties. In obsessional states, the soldier realizes the morbid nature of his symptoms and even that his fears are at their root.[39] Even so, his tremors, palpitations, stammers, tics, etc., cannot be controlled. Eventually the soldier is likely to take refuge in some type of hysterical reaction which allows him to escape psychic responsibility for his physical symptoms.

CHARACTER DISORDERS: : This set of symptoms is somewhat misnamed, for it implies that somehow the soldier's character has been disordered by conscious action. This is not the case. What is meant is a condition in which the problems of stress have become so deeply seated that they have become part of the soldier's personality; this condition is extremely difficult to reverse. Character disorders include stable obsessional traits in which the soldier becomes fixated on certain actions or things; paranoid trends accompanied by irascibility, depression, and anxiety, often taking on the tone of threats to his safety; schizoid trends leading to hypersensitivity and isolation; epileptoid character reactions accompanied by periodic rages; the development of extreme dramatic religiosity; and finally degeneration into a psychopathic personality.[40] What has happened to the soldier is an altering of his fundamental personality. While some of these alterations can be reversed, all too commonly they accompany the soldier for the rest of his life.

It is important to understand that some symptoms of stress will develop in almost all soldiers in battle. Moreover, while not all soldiers will collapse from this stress, almost all will suffer some degree of combat debilitation—some lessening of their ability to fight—as a consequence. Table 1 lists psychiatric symptoms and the approximate frequency of occurrence manifested by Israeli soldiers in the 1982 Lebanon war. While many soldiers had multiple symptoms, it is clear from the available information that the range and frequency of symptoms is very great indeed. It is also evident that soldiers tend to suffer clusters of symptoms. These clusters, while evident to some degree in every war for which there are available data, have tended to emerge in specific forms in different wars. Table 2 presents the most prevalent symptoms which emerged in each conflict since World War I. While the data are not included in the table, many of the same clusters emerged in the Civil War as well, although under different names. Tragically, the most common symptom to manifest itself in all wars, including those in Roman times for which there are no statistical data, is also the most serious. Conversion reactions, a condition in which the soldier "converts" his fear into a physical debilitation such as

TABLE 1   Psychiatric Symptoms Reported by Israeli Soldiers in
the 1982 Lebanon War

Symptom	% Reporting
Anxiety	56
Depressive affect	38
Sleep disturbances	34
Fear—focused and diffuse	34
Social estrangement-detachment	24
Conversion reactions	22
Crying	21
Decreased appetite	19
Headaches	19
Exhaustion, fatigue	17
Psychomotor disturbances	17
Disturbing dreams-memories	17
Tremors	13
Confusion, concentration problems	13
Speech impairment	12
Dissociative states	11
Irritability	11
Explosive aggressive behavior	11
Memory impairment	11
Noise sensitivity–startle reactions	10

Note: Percentages reflect those soldiers in the IDF who reported each symptom. Since soldiers may have suffered more than one symptom, the percentages do not add to 100.

Source: Gregory Belenky, Israeli Battle Shock Casualties: 1973 and 1982 (Washington, D.C.: Walter Reed Army Institute of Research Report, 1983), p. 12.

blindness, paralysis, etc., remains the most common reaction to long-term exposure to battle stress.

Conclusion

The foregoing analysis of the symptoms of acute and gradual battle shock by no means exhausts the manifestations which emerge among soldiers subjected to prolonged battle stress. The mind has shown itself infinitely capable of bringing about any number of combinations of symptoms and then, to make matters worse, burying them deep in the soldier's psyche so that even the overt manifestations become symp-

TABLE 2 **Symptom Clusters in Various Wars**

Symptoms	WWI	WWII	Vietnam	Arab-Israeli Wars 1973	1982
Depressive affect	X			X	X
Fear—focused and diffuse	X			X	X
Noise sensitivity	X				
Tremors	X				
Psychomotor disturbance	X				
Conversion reaction	X	X		X	X
Confusion, aprosexia	X				
Dissociative states	X			X	
Anxiety		X		X	X
Nightmares		X		X	
Exhaustion, fatigue		X			
Decreased appetite		X			
Gastrointestinal		X			
Headaches		X			
Sleep disturbances		X		X	X
Constricted affect			X		
Social estrangement			X		X
Discipline problems			X		
Explosive behavior			X		
Drug abuse			X		

Note: Each X represents the most common symptoms reported by psychiatric casualties in each war.

Source: Belenky, op. cit., p. 10.

toms of deeper symptoms of even deeper underlying causes.

What this all adds up to is that war exacts a terrible cost in human emotions quite apart from the usual costs calculated in terms of dollars, dead, and wounded. And it is a cost which every soldier will eventually pay if he is exposed long enough to the horrors of the battlefield. Weakness or cowardice has nothing to do with the probability that a soldier will collapse under the strain of battle. It is not man that is too weak; it is the conduct of war that imposes too great a strain for the sane to endure. And there is no way to make the problem of battle shock go away; it is an inevitable part of the game. Indeed, what the statistical analysis of the frequency of battle shock clearly demonstrates is that it is a more frequently occurring factor than even death.

What is even more horrifying is the persistence of romantic notions of war in the face of the facts. Because most Americans have never personally known the touch of war except lightly, they seem to be all the more prone to cast war in romantic terms. Fed a steady diet of movies and television programs which portray war unrealistically, the average citizen comes to believe that these impressions of war are genuine. There is no deep understanding of the real tragedies which occur in battle. So the myth persists that those who collapse under the strain of battle are somehow weak or cowardly or the exception to the rule. And that may be the worst self-delusion of all.

4

Psychiatry in War

Psychiatry, in one form or another, is as old as man himself. It emerged in its most basic form the first time one human being attempted to help another deal with personal anguish. Men have always faced many of the personal problems and uncertainties—death of a child, loss of a spouse, fear of the unknown, an awareness of one's mortality—that modern men face, and surely early man, in dealing with these problems, suffered from the same pain and anguish that we do. Moreover, early man's understanding of his environment and his own behavior was so inexact that he resorted to religion to deal with his fears and ignorance. The first shamans earned their keep in primitive societies by providing explanations and rituals that enabled man to deal with his environment and his personal anguish. Early man, no less than we, dealt with forces that he could not understand or control, and he attempted to come to grips with his vulnerability by trying to bring some order to his universe.

Those who could interpret and explain that universe, in whatever terms, were the precursors of our psychiatrists.

Psychiatry is a different discipline from psychology, but the differences are becoming increasingly narrowed. Psychiatrists have historically been defined as "healers of the mind," whereas psychologists are defined as "those who study the mind." This distinction, based on the difference between medical doctors who treated mental illness and scholars who studied it, has become less useful in the modern era, especially in military psychiatry, as psychologists have carved out a significant role as clinicians treating those suffering from emotional problems. Traditionally, psychiatry was closely tied to the general practice of medicine and has its roots in attempts to link human behavior to the physiology of the brain. With the recognition that human beings often suffer from purely emotional problems which have no physiological explanation, clinical psychology has come into its own. Most of those who deal with the problem of battle stress in the military establishments of the world are psychologists, not psychiatrists. Both have become "healers of the mind."

Psychiatry had its beginnings in man's attempt to explain strange behavior in his fellow men, behavior that was initially attributed to forces outside the afflicted individual. Whether the problem was death, disease, cowardice in battle, debilitating fear in war or on the hunt, its causes were attributable to larger forces that man could not control. Accordingly, the earliest explanations for mental illness—as recorded in ancient Babylon in 2750 B.C.—attributed it to the anger of powerful deities whom man, through his immoral behavior, had angered. Since men seem incapable of living in a world in which they feel totally helpless, early psychiatrists attributed madness—and even defeat in battle—to the faults in man's character. Both Egyptian and Hebraic concepts of mental illness (and even physical illness) were rooted in the notion of individual sin. It was not until the rise of Greek medicine that it was possible for ancient psychiatrists to break away from the Egyptian and Hebraic notions that sin caused madness. The Greeks were the first to bring to the study of medicine—and the physiology of the brain—the systematic use of reason joined with empirical observation that led to the conclusion that madness was caused by physical and emotional forces within the individual and not by diabolical outside forces.

Modern psychiatry has its roots in the Greek empirical method of medical observation. Greek physicians studied the brain in detail. At the same time, however, Greek medicine was based on a view of human nature that permitted the development of the theory of personality, first put forth by Plato, which attributed mental problems to purely emotional causes. Thus, the Greeks were the first to develop the dualism which still characterizes psychiatry. One view saw human behavior as rooted in the physiology of the brain, a view evident today in the study of brain chemistry. A second view rooted human behavior in the mind, which produced its own reality—perceptions, emotions, etc.—quite apart from the physiology of the brain. This view is evident in modern-day Freudian psychiatry. The tension between these two perspectives accompanied the development of psychiatry through the ages.

Psychiatric thought from the time of the Greeks to the fall of Rome was characterized by a predominant emphasis on physiological explanations for mental illness. This view, biological psychiatry, was eclipsed in the Dark Ages (fifth century–twelfth century) by more irrational explanations for madness. Much of what passed for psychiatry in this period was essentially doctrinal, formed and enforced by a single universal Catholic Church. By the thirteenth century it had degenerated to the point where mental illness was viewed as the product of demonic possession brought on by the sins of the sufferer. The most common explanation for madness was possession caused by witchcraft, in which the sufferer willingly allowed himself to be possessed by demons and other spirits of the devil. Because the person possessed had willingly brought about his own evil condition, the only appropriate treatment was torture, recantation, and burning at the stake.

The Renaissance saw the reemergence of the traditional Greek notion of human behavior based on the physiology of the brain. The anatomical studies of men like Leonardo da Vinci helped propel a rapidly developing discipline of medical investigation. This return to more empirical methods was resisted at every turn by the established religions, and throughout the Renaissance the investigations and practices of medical men often resulted in their being executed for heresy.

It was the Enlightenment of the seventeenth century, with its emphasis on scientific investigation, that gradually moved psychiatry away from purely emotional explanations for mental illness. By the eighteenth and early nineteenth centuries, medical science had developed to the point where man's knowledge of the brain seemed to offer the promise of dealing with mental illness through an understanding of its physiology.

The eighteenth and nineteenth centuries saw the full development of this view into the discipline of biological psychiatry. On the battlefields of the Civil War, the Crimean War, the Franco-Prussian War, and the Russo-Japanese War of 1904–5, biological psychiatry gained and maintained predominance in explaining human behavior. Physicians who were in attendance at each of these wars saw them as a great opportunity to learn more about the brain and its influence on human behavior. While the predominant effect of these wars on the study of medicine was the birth of the field of neurology, they also produced the first military psychiatrists. Biological psychiatry would maintain its dominant position in the discipline until Sigmund Freud in the twentieth century offered an alternative explanation for human behavior based primarily on the emotions. At present, psychiatry in general and military psychiatry in particular are

again divided over alternative ways of explaining and dealing with mental phenomena, with psychiatrists often holding to the biological view and psychologists to the Freudian
view.

Military psychiatry is a recent development, dating only
from the Civil War, when neurologists made a systematic
attempt to link damage to the brain to emotional behavior.
In a strict sense, however, military psychiatry did not emerge
as a separate discipline until the Russo-Japanese War. While
psychiatry over the centuries reflected two different views
of human behavior and mental illness, the military establishments of the West, from the time of the Greeks until
World War I, proceeded in near-total ignorance of the debate. For military commanders the problem of fear in battle
had a more pressing urgency and was dealt with in more
direct ways.

Military perceptions of why men collapse in battle were
formed more than two thousand years ago in the military
experiences of classical Greece (450 B.C.). The Greeks believed that performance in battle was a function of the character of the soldier. Greek military literature emphasized the
connection between moral character and military training
and heroism in battle. Heroes were men who controlled their
fears; cowards succumbed to them; that was the only relevant criterion for assessing soldierly performance. So strongly
did the Greeks hold this view that for almost four hundred
years they resisted the adoption of superior military technologies—with which they were quite familiar after their
wars with the Persians—on the grounds that to adopt weapons of greater range and lethality would destroy the distinction between heroes and cowards. After all, if a hail of
arrows from Persian bows could kill at a distance of two
hundred yards, thus eliminating hand-to-hand combat, then
war had become too indiscriminate, killing heroes and cowards alike by mere chance. In order to sustain the view that
moral character distinguished the good soldier, the Greeks

refused to change their tactics or adopt the new "immoral" weaponry of their enemies. The fact that these weapons were more effective mattered not one whit.

The conviction that the soldier's character was the most important element in deciding performance under fire persisted for centuries. In World War I, French soldiers were expected to overcome the Germans' technological advantages by sheer force of courage and will. French *élan* was expected to be the crucial difference. The result was that thousands of soldiers went over the top and walked slowly to their deaths into the teeth of enemy machine guns and artillery. Any sane calculation of war at that time would have concluded that the technology of war—the objective circumstances of the battlefield—had become more important than heroism or courage in gaining victory. Yet the myth persisted with devastating effects. On July 1, 1916, the British Army launched the battle of the Somme. In less than four hours, 52,000 Englishmen had been killed and wounded. Many of their officers went over the top carrying only swagger sticks. And still they went, wave after wave, to meet their inevitable deaths. The myth of moral character as the dominant factor in a soldier's performance is no less alive today than it was in 1916 and no less false.

If there were no military psychiatrists before the Civil War, it is nonetheless true that earlier armies had sought to deal with the major problem of breakdown in battle in ways that are familiar to modern military psychiatrists. If mental collapse was a function of poor moral character, the task of military commanders was to prevent it. Armies adopted a number of measures to reduce manpower losses caused by battle shock.

The obvious way of reducing battle shock was to emphasize programs to instill moral character. Greek and Roman generals sought to toughen their armies by strict regimens of military discipline and hardship. Spartan soldiers from boyhood were not given enough to eat; nor were they allowed to wear sandals. They were trained to endure physical hardship and thus develop the will to overcome it. Another method was to use the soldier's sense of self-respect to overcome fear. Greek and Roman armies made great efforts to form military units comprised of men from the same town or city. The Greeks even made it a practice to station homosexuals and their lovers in the same units. These policies increased the social cohesion of the fighting group, and similar techniques were used right through World Wars I and II. In World War I, the British always tried to raise regiments on a county basis, as did the Canadians, Germans, and French, and some British regiments were even raised from single occupations, such as mining and longshoring. Throughout World War II, German regiments were still drawn from the same city or town.

A common method of controlling a soldier's fear was to convince him that the costs of behaving improperly were always greater and far more certain than any gains achieved by behaving improperly under fire. Harsh discipline, including whipping, starvation, and the threat of execution, were commonplace solutions among the armies of the seventeenth and eighteenth centuries. It was commonly held that men must fear their officers more than death from the enemy, an injunction of Prussia's Frederick the Great, the father of the German Army. As late as the 1870s the American Army used tattooing and branding as punishment for cowardice. In World War I, French units which refused to fire on the German trenches were subject to artillery bombardments from their own guns. After the mutiny of French divisions on the Western Front in 1917, men of the rebellious divisions which refused to attack were selected at random and publicly executed. British, French, and Canadian armies in World War I stationed battle police just to the rear of the front lines with instructions to shoot soldiers who turned away from the fight.

Other solutions to the problem were found in religious faith and ritual. Medieval commanders never went into battle until they had heard Mass and communion was delivered to their troops. Priests have always been in attendance at battles, usually urging the soldiers to fight harder "for God and country." In the Vietnam War, it will be recalled, Cardinal Cooke stood on the flight deck of an American aircraft carrier blessing the pilots as they took off on bombing runs against targets in North Vietnam. Attending a religious service before battle is still a commonplace ritualistic defense against fear. Before going into battle, Moslem soldiers in Iran commonly attend a final religious service at which they are given a small plastic key to open the doors of paradise after they die in battle. And the impact of ritualistic practices should not be underestimated, especially in a world that has been treated to a number of attacks by terrorists who have demonstrated their willingness to die in the service of a cause.

For more than a thousand years armies have used chemical means to steel the will of their soldiers against fear. The Vikings of the ninth century routinely used chemical stimulants made from deer urine. British soldiers, to this day, are entitled by military regulation to a stiff jigger of rum before going into battle. On the field of Waterloo in 1815, rum made the difference for a number of heavily engaged British units. In the Philippine insurrection at the turn of the century, the Mauro Indians took drugs prior to battle. A number of southwestern American Indian tribes used drugs before fighting. American soldiers in Vietnam stiffened their courage with marijuana or "skin-popping" diluted heroin or opium. Soviet soldiers in World War II were routinely given drugs made from herbal compounds to calm their nerves. Although modern armies may be exploring more sophisticated chemical means to control fear, the chemical solution has a long historical precedent.

What these attempts to prevent battle stress have in common is the fact that they have not succeeded very well. The reason is simply that the character of a soldier has very little to do with his ability to endure the stress of battle. While some men collapse sooner than others, the critical variables are the objective conditions of battle to which the soldier is exposed. Despite the best efforts of military establishments to stem manpower loss from battle shock, the fact is that armies always suffered great reductions in combat power as soldiers became debilitated through fear, either to the point where they collapsed and had to be evacuated or, more commonly, to the point where they were so frightened that they could not function. At the battle of Gettysburg, for example, hundreds of rifles were found which had several balls and charges stuffed into their muzzles. Their owners were so frightened that they continued to load the rifles and simply forgot to pull the trigger after each load. Moreover, as the killing power of weaponry increases, the number of soldiers who will certainly suffer battle shock symptoms is increasing at an alarming rate. What steps can military psychiatrists take to deal with the problem? In order to answer that question, it is important to understand how military psychiatry has attempted to deal with the problem in the modern era.

Military Psychiatry in the Civil War

The Civil War was the most destructive war in American history, killing and wounding more American soldiers than any war before or since. Psychiatry was still in its infancy, and although some psychiatrists recognized that men could become debilitated from purely emotional forces, the major thrust of the discipline was characterized by the study of brain physiology and the attempt to link disruptions of that physiology to behavioral disorders. In the United States there were fewer than a dozen mental hospitals and none for patients who developed emotional disorders in war or military life. Care of the mentally ill rested in the hands of the handful of superintendents of these mental asylums. The movement for humane treatment of the mentally ill, which had begun in France fifty years before, was just beginning to take root in the United States. Within the military itself, there were no psychiatrists at all, and the military continued to take the traditional view that soldiers who broke down in battle were cowards or had a "weak" character. American military psychiatry by 1860 had not come very far since the Revolutionary War and was, in many ways, considerably behind the development of the discipline in Europe.

It is easily forgotten just how primitive battlefield medicine was in the Civil War. Operations were performed without anesthesia, surgeons rarely if ever washed before examining open wounds, and infection was regarded as a normal and beneficial part of the healing process. It was a war of medical horrors. At the battle of Gettysburg, Union Army surgeons collapsed from exhaustion because they had to amputate so many limbs—most of them while the patient remained conscious! In this context, the lack of trained psychiatrists to deal with emotional and behavioral problems could only be seen as a minor problem.

The Civil War became the progenitor of modern war and saw the first use of new and horribly destructive weapons. It also saw their employment on a scale heretofore unimagined. It was on the battlefields of Antietam, Gettysburg, and Chancellorsville that troops made their first headlong frontal assaults against repeating rifles and pistols whose rates of fire caused thousands of casualties. The Civil War also saw masses of men attacking frontally against massed rifled artillery guns whose repertoire of caliber and shot caused horrible casualties. The use of the delayed timed artillery fuse which allowed artillery rounds to burst above the heads of advancing soldiers increased the number of head wounds dramatically. The lack of any protective headgear also contributed to the number of head and neurological injuries. The introduction of telescopic sights and rifles with spiral barreled rifling greatly increased the accuracy of massed rifle fire. The Gatling gun, a somewhat basic but nonetheless effective machine gun, made its appearance with devastating impact. The technology of war was making the battlefield much more lethal than it had ever been, and the predictable result was an increase in the number of dead, wounded, and psychiatric casualties. The Civil War marked man's first step on the road to truly modern war.

Almost immediately medical officers had to deal with the problem of psychiatric casualties. Since the War Department had rejected the offer of a group of superintendents of insane asylums to treat the problem on the battlefields, treatment fell to surgeons. The experience gained by these surgeons with psychiatric cases led to the birth in the United States of the field of neurology and hardened even further the tendency of medical practitioners of the day to regard mental problems among soldiers as due to damaged physiology of the brain. Nonetheless, even these neurologists had to admit that there was a range of disorders which afflicted soldiers that had no sound physiological explanation, and by 1863, at their urging, the first military hospital in the United States devoted to the treatment of psychiatric casualties was founded.

The most common psychiatric condition with which medical officers had to deal was nostalgia, a cluster of symptoms resulting from emotional and physical fatigue that made it impossible for the soldier to continue fighting. Moreover, they also began to encounter a range of symptoms which mimicked different diseases but for which any sound physical cause was lacking. Thus, for every hundred soldiers discharged for "nervous disease," 28.3 manifested a condition that mimicked epilepsy and 20.8 a condition that mimicked paralysis.[1] Today we know that these symptoms are conversion reactions produced by strong affective fear. No less than 6 percent of all soldiers discharged for medical reasons were released for "general insanity" brought on by the war.

Psychiatric symptoms became so common that field commanders, with the support of medical doctors, pleaded with the War Department to provide some form of screening to eliminate recruits susceptible to psychiatric breakdown. In 1863, the Union Army instituted the world's first psychiatric screening program of recruits. It didn't help any more than it did in World War I, and the number of psychiatric cases continued to increase.

It must be remembered that only a handful of physicians in the country had any experience in dealing with psychiatric patients whose conditions were brought on by emotional turbulence. For the most part these were superintendents of civilian mental asylums, none of whom saw service during the war. Accordingly, military physicians were usually at a loss in dealing with cases of "insanity." In the first three years of the war soldiers who became "insane" were mustered out on the spot. This was a particularly cruel solution, although it had long historical precedent in the armies of Europe. Insane soldiers in the Union and Confederate armies were often escorted to the main gate of a military camp and turned loose. Others were put on trains with no supervision, the name of their hometown or state pinned to their tunics. Others were left to wander about the countryside until they died from exposure or starvation. By 1863, the number of insane or shocked soldiers wandering around the country was so great that there was a public outcry. In that year the military finally forbade the discharge of insane soldiers. Instead, they were sent to the newly established military hospital for the insane.

While no hard figures exist, by the end of the Civil War almost six thousand soldiers had been discharged for the psychiatric condition of nostalgia alone, and this only in the Union Army. The number suffering from "epilepsy" and hysterical paralysis was probably twice as large, and the number discharged for insanity reached several thousand. It is fair to assume that similar proportions were evident on the Confederate side, but there are no surviving data to confirm this. Although the problem of psychiatric breakdown reached major proportions by war's end, not a single article or book on the subject was published in the postwar years. The military psychiatric hospital was closed, and the government made no effort to deal with the psychiatrically wounded by involving the doctors who treated mental illness in the civilian community. The problem was conveniently forgotten, and except for the advances in neurology, battle shock and psychiatric debilitation were no longer of concern to the military. This failure to learn from experience would return to haunt the American Army when it took the field in World War I.

Russo-Japanese War

If the Americans were prepared to forget their experience with battle shock, the Russians were not. The Russian military had encountered psychiatric casualties induced by the stress of war in the Crimean War of 1853–56. A significant number of British soldiers were also driven insane in the Crimea by the tremendous firepower—mostly the indirect fire of artillery barrages unleashed by siege mortars. However, Russian military doctors—unlike the British, who were drawn mostly from the civilian medical establishment rather than from the military—remained interested in battle shock after the war. Their interest was further stimulated by similar evidence of battle shock in the American Civil War and in the Franco-Prussian War of 1870. By the time of the Russo-Japanese War of 1904–5, the Russians were prepared to attempt to deal with the problem in a very modern and sophisticated way. Indeed, their attempts to diagnose and cure battle shock in 1905 represent the birth of military psychiatry.

The first army in history to determine that mental collapse was a consequence of the stress of war and to regard it as a true medical condition was the Russian Army of 1905. It was also the first army to attempt to prevent it and treat it. The Russians laid many of the foundations of modern military psychiatry.

During the Russo-Japanese War, Russian Army physicians diagnosed and treated approximately two thousand casualties which they attributed directly to battle shock. However, the number of soldiers complaining of lesser psychiatric symptoms was very much larger, so large in fact that as the war progressed, field medical facilities were unable to handle the load. As the numbers grew, many psychiatric casualties were evacuated to the rear and turned over to the Russian Red Cross for institutionalized treatment and care. The numbers reached such alarming proportions that they eventually overwhelmed the home-front resources. The Russian experience with such large numbers of psychiatric casualties shipped to the rear provided the first modern example of "evacuation syndrome." When soldiers began to realize that "insane" soldiers were being relieved of combat duty, the number of psychiatric casualties increased dramatically as soldiers began to manifest psychiatric symptoms to escape the horrors of the front. Paradoxically, it was the Russian willingness to recognize and deal with psychiatric casualties that produced even more such casualties among the troops.

The Russian Army was the first to place psychiatrists near the front line. Most of these psychiatrists, however, came from civilian mental hospitals and had no training in dealing with psychiatric problems in a military environment. It would not be until World War I that there was any such thing as a "military psychiatrist." In the 1905 war the Russians established psychiatric dispensaries staffed with psychiatrists and other medical personnel near the front lines and had their own transport for dealing specifically with psychiatric casualties. Surgical casualties were treated through the normal medical channels, while psychiatric casualties were sent to the psychiatric dispensaries. The field staff in the dispensaries included a psychiatrist or a neurologist who dealt with brain injuries, a physician's assistant, and a complement of three medics. Armies of the West would not attain this degree of organizational definition for dealing with psychiatric casualties until 1917.

The major Russian contribution to military psychiatry was their institutionalization of the principle of proximity, or forward treatment. The Russians felt that a number of psychiatric problems which afflicted soldiers could be readily cured if treated rapidly within the battle zone and as close to the front as possible. Experience in both world wars proved them to be right, and today the principle of forward treatment remains the bedrock of military psychiatry in all armies. However, it was a lesson that was lost on the armies of the West until 1916–17 and, once the war ended, it was promptly forgotten during the interwar period. It reappeared toward the end of World War II, when it was used by the American Army. Forward treatment was used by the Americans in Korea and Vietnam with considerable success. After the 1973 Arab-Israeli war, the large number of Israeli psychiatric casualties prompted the Israelis to send a number of experts to the United States to study our methods of dealing with psychiatric casualties. The result was the development of a system which closely parallels the American system and is still in use today. The basis of that system is forward treatment.

The Russian Army was also the first to establish a central psychiatric hospital immediately behind the lines, in the town of Harbin, Manchuria. That hospital recorded between forty-three and ninety psychiatric admissions a day. Of these, only a few were quickly cured and returned to the line. The rest remained in the hospital for about fifteen days and were subjected to a variety of treatments. If they did not recover in that time, they were evacuated by train to Moscow, a trip which often took forty days on the single-track railroad. Evacuation of psychiatric patients to Moscow was attended by a surgeon and a small staff of physician's assistants. By the end of the war the Russian Medical Corps had several special trains exclusively for psychiatric patients. These trains had isolation compartments, restraint rooms, and barred windows.

Although the Russians were right in treating psychiatric casualties close to the front with the goal of returning them to the fight, the rates of successful recovery suggest that they were not very successful. Of the 275 officers admitted to the psychiatric hospital at Harbin for a fifteen-day period, only 54 recovered sufficiently to be sent back to the fighting and 221 were evacuated to Moscow. Of the 1,072 enlisted soldiers treated at Harbin, only 51 recovered and were returned to duty and 983 were evacuated to the rear.[2]

In 1905 the Russians quickly recognized the problem of secondary gain: the farther a soldier suffering from psychiatric symptoms was removed from the front lines, the less likely he was to recover. This phenomenon is called secondary gain because a soldier suffering from psychiatric difficulties actually "gains" by being relieved from the fighting and will unconsciously maintain his symptoms out of fear of being sent back. Thus, the farther a soldier is removed from the front lines, the less willing he is to confront his symptoms and the more difficult they are to reverse. The result is to force the symptoms deeper into the psyche. During World War II, Allied armies lost thousands of troops to psychiatric symptoms simply because patients were evacuated far to the rear. Once there, they had a strong interest in sustaining their symptoms in order to avoid being returned to the fighting. By 1917, the experience of most Western armies had confirmed the Russian experience with secondary gain in 1905.

During the Russo-Japanese War, Russian psychiatrists made very significant advances in clinically linking battle stress with a number of somatic symptoms. When the hundreds of case records of psychiatric patients during that war are analyzed, it is clear that the Russians were far ahead of any other army in being able to describe battle stress casualties using diagnostic categories that are quite modern. Indeed, many of them are still used today by other armies. Russian psychiatrists recorded cases of hysterical excitement, confused states, fugue states, hysterical blindness, surdomutism, local paralysis, and neurasthenia. Since most Russian psychiatry was derived from German biological psychiatry, Russian doctors tended to define these symptoms in purely physiological terms. Thus, a wide range of symptoms which today we know are directly attributable to emotional turbulence were attributed by Russian psychiatrists to traumatic psychosis of organic origins. In 1905, 55.6 percent of Russian battle stress casualties were diagnosed as being due to traumatic damage to the brain.[3] By World War I, the major tendency of Western military psychiatry was still to regard stress reactions as due to physiological damage to the brain.

By World War I, the Russian Army was the most experienced army in dealing with the clinical problems of battle shock. It was the first to specify categories of psychiatric problems seen to be directly related to the stress of battle, it was the first to institutionalize forward treatment, it was the first to develop a complete theory of what caused battle stress, and it was the first army to deal with evacuation syndrome and secondary gain. For the most part, however, the lessons of the 1904–5 war were ignored in the West, most particularly in the United States. It would take the experience of World War I before the armies of the West, confronted with their own huge losses for psychiatric reasons, would begin to attempt to find ways to deal with the problem.

World War I

The outbreak of World War I immediately produced large numbers of psychiatric casualties. Within Allied armies, military psychiatry was almost unknown as a functioning discipline and, more important, few Allied physicians knew or recalled the Russian experience with psychiatric casualties only ten years earlier. As a consequence, the medical establishments of the West thought they were dealing with an entirely new phenomenon in which "the present war is the first in which the functional nervous diseases (shell-shock) have constituted a major medico-military problem."[4] It was believed that most psychiatric cases were the consequence of new weapons, most particularly large-caliber artillery. Mental debilitation was widely believed to be caused by the concussive effects of shelling which produced a disruption in the physiology of the brain. Emotionally rooted explanations—such as fear and anxiety—were regarded as highly conjectural and never granted wide acceptance.

For the first two years of the war the French and British simply evacuated psychiatric cases far to the rear. British casualties were transported to medical hospitals in England, with the predictable result that few recovered completely and almost none were returned to the fighting. In France, the early practice of evacuating psychiatric casualties to civilian hospitals deep in the country had to be abandoned by 1917 when opposition to the war made it politically unwise to do so, since the presence of returned casualties tended to feed wartime opposition. By 1917 both the French and the British were treating psychiatric cases close to the front with the hope of eventually returning the cured to the fighting.

After the outbreak of war, stories filtered back to the United States about new types of mental diseases which were afflicting Allied soldiers. The American Army had no program at all for treating psychiatric casualties and very few psychiatrists in its ranks. Its only experience with psychiatric casualties had come ten years before when American soldiers stationed with General John J. Pershing on the Mexican border were shown to be suffering a rate of mental illness three times higher than the rate exhibited by the entire state of New York![5] It was not until 1917, just prior to the American entry into the war, that the War Department began to take an interest in psychiatric casualties.

At the urging of a coalition of civilian mental health professionals organized as the National Committee for Mental Hygiene, a committee was established to consult with the Surgeon General to create a structure for dealing with psychiatric problems in the military forces. Dr. Thomas Salmon, a member of the committee, visited England to learn firsthand how the British and the French were dealing with the problem. His recommendations became the basis for establishing an American corps of psychiatrists to deal with psychiatric casualties. When the United States entered the war, the number of American psychiatric casualties grew to significant proportions.

The American military began to train doctors and supporting staff in military psychiatry. By war's end, the U.S. military had 693 psychiatrists in service with 263 stationed overseas.[6] Psychiatric staffs were organized in each division and small psychiatric hospitals capable of handling thirty patients at a time were set up near the front lines. Larger hospitals were established farther to the rear but still within a reasonable distance. The Americans were following established Russian and German practice in using forward treatment of psychiatric casualties.

An important element in the treatment of psychiatric casualties eventually became known as the principle of expectancy. Psychiatric patients were to be treated as close to the front as possible and, in principle, all casualties were screened at a clearing station near the lines to determine who could be treated near the front and who was to be shipped to rear-area hospitals. Whether near the front or in the rear, medical personnel conveyed to the soldier that as soon as he recovered he would be expected to return to his unit. Being separated from his unit, he was told, was detrimental to him and to his comrades who wanted him back. In World War II, the principle of expectancy was found to be very important in preventing a patient from developing secondary gain.

American military psychiatrists found that most psychiatric casualties were not suffering from physiological damage to the brain. Emotion, not brain damage, was most often causing the full range of psychiatric symptoms. They also found that many symptoms would disappear with a few days' rest, food, and a respite from battle. The American Army in World War I never made as extensive use of such therapies as hypnosis and electroshock as other armies did. And the success rate was fairly good; about 40 percent of psychiatric casualties were returned to the fighting; however, many of them became psychiatric casualties again.

While the American strategy for dealing with the problem worked fairly well at first, by the time American troops became engaged in the war in large numbers, the nature of the war had changed. Trench warfare had given way to a war of movement and maneuver. This meant that psychiatric treatment facilities were unable to remain close to the front, since the armies moved rapidly forward in one offensive after another, and so the medical service could not prevent large numbers of psychiatric casualties from being evacuated in normal medical channels to points far in the rear. Many of them were evacuated along with surgical casualties, effectively bypassing the psychiatric clearing stations.

By war's end, the American psychiatric medical structure had only limited experience in dealing with the practical problems of holding and returning psychiatric casualties to the front. Worse, the American Army began to draw the wrong lessons from its experiences. Although it knew that most psychiatric casualties were not caused by damage to the brain, it continued to believe that men collapsed in battle primarily because they were of weak character. The solution, therefore, was to reduce the number of conscripts with a predisposition to collapse. Because most psychiatric practitioners who served during World War I had drawn their experience from civilian hospitals, where they treated the insane, and because a number of symptoms exhibited by soldiers under fire paralleled the symptoms manifested by their civilian patients, they, too, drew the wrong lesson.[7]

They should have learned that all men are subject to psychiatric collapse, simply as sane men reacting to insane circumstances. The principal lesson drawn, however, was that soldiers had to be rigorously screened for predisposition to breakdown. When the "unfit" were eliminated, it was reasonably expected, the problem would largely disappear. It was the wrong conclusion. Although the Army did benefit from its establishment of permanent psychiatric hospitals within its medical structure and the presence in each division of a psychiatrist, for the most part the lessons of forward treatment and expectancy were lost in the effort to develop exact psychiatric tests which could be used by draft boards to eliminate those with a predisposition to collapse. The idea that psychiatric collapse is the reaction of even sane men when placed under great enough stress was given no credence. World War II would finally teach the American military just how wrong it had been.

World War II

Given the lessons that the American Army drew from World War I, it is not surprising that the main effort to reduce psychiatric casualties in World War II was focused on screening draftees in order to weed out those thought to be predisposed to psychiatric collapse. The Army used the best available psychiatric tests and rejected no fewer than 1.6 million for military service, a psychiatric rejection rate of 18.5 percent, nearly seven times higher than in World War I.[8] If the screening process was valid, then the American Army should not have suffered serious problems of psychiatric casualties. Unfortunately, the rate at which soldiers in World War II were admitted to psychiatric hospitals was double the World War I rate and separations from service for mental and emotional reasons increased almost seven times over the rate in World War I. Psychiatric casualties constituted the single largest category of disability discharges in World War II.[9]

Because the American military put so much faith in screening out the unfit, it made little provision for dealing with psychiatric casualties in the first two years of the war. In general, through 1943 there were no effective divisional psychiatric facilities in the field, and the common practice was to evacuate all psychiatric casualties far to the rear. The result was a medical disaster.

In the early days of the Tunisian and Sicilian campaigns in 1943, the rates of psychiatric casualties were staggering. Some divisions suffered 100% psychiatric casualties. Whole battalions became debilitated because of stress-related problems. On average, 35 percent of all nonfatal casualties during this period were psychiatric. Worse, because they could not be treated near the front, they were evacuated ninety or more miles to the rear to theater or corps level. As a result, no more than 3 percent of the men evacuated ever returned to combat. A report published in 1944 records that nearly all the men in rifle battalions not otherwise disabled by wounds became psychiatric casualties in the North African theater![10]

By 1944, it became apparent to military medical authorities that every soldier exposed to combat was subject to psychiatric collapse. In the Volturno, Rapido, and Cassino actions, medical personnel began to notice that even old combat veterans, many of whom had received decorations for bravery, were beginning to collapse under the stress ("old soldier's syndrome"). What finally drove home the point was that the Air Force was suffering high rates of psychiatric debilitation among its air crews, men who had been specially selected for their intelligence and stability and who had been given long periods of stress training while at pilot school.

By late 1943, the military began to recognize that psychiatric breakdown was too common to be regarded as abnormal. The diagnostic name for psychiatric collapse was changed from "psychoneurosis" to "exhaustion," a change which indicated that there was nothing particularly shameful about a man collapsing under the stress of battle.

Having realized that it had made a mistake in believing that recruit screening would make the problem of psychiatric casualties largely disappear, the Army found itself unprepared in doctrine and resources to deal with a growing problem that threatened the combat power of the American Army. There were acute shortages of psychiatrists throughout the Army and the shortage of psychiatrists for division-level service was never truly solved during the war. Worse, training for psychiatric assistants and line medics was almost nonexistent. By 1944 the military had succeeded in reestablishing a World War I hierarchical structure for treatment, with facilities at division, army, and theater levels. Because these facilities were never fully staffed until late in the war, they never functioned even as well as they did in World War I. More importantly, the ability of the system to function well depended heavily on the medics and physician's assistants stationed at company and battalion aid stations. Since these personnel often had no training in screening psychiatric casualties, for months the system continued to evacuate casualties who should have been held at battalion or division and returned to the fighting. Nonetheless, in the last days of the war, the system began to function fairly well just as the prospect of victory began to reduce the number of psychiatric casualties in the ranks. The return rates of psychiatric casualties began to rise, but never equaled the return rates of World War I.

After the war, the military medical departments began to collect and analyze the data relevant to their experience with psychiatric casualties. It was finally determined that psychiatric breakdown was not the result of a predisposition to collapse. It was at last accepted that battle stress would break all soldiers exposed to it long enough, a fact buttressed by the finding that over time there was no difference in the rate of psychiatric breakdown between new and veteran soldiers.[11] In 1948 Roy Swank and Walter Marchand, two civilian psychiatrists, detailed for the first time the dynamics of psychiatric collapse, pointing out that after thirty-five days of sustained combat no less than 98 percent of combat soldiers manifested adverse psychiatric symptoms.[12] The principles of forward treatment and expectancy, which had first emerged in World War I, became part of official military doctrine, and psychiatrists were permanently assigned to division medical facilities. In its training doctrines, however, the Army persisted in the belief that trained soldiers could be made to withstand the horrors of the battlefield for long periods. The military had not yet realized that war itself was changing radically.

Korea and Vietnam

The outbreak of war in Korea in June 1950 found the military relatively well prepared to deal with psychiatric casualties. For the first two months of the war, as American units were repeatedly defeated and driven back to the Pusan perimeter, psychiatric casualties skyrocketed to rates two and three times higher than had been observed during World War II. Once the front had stabilized, however, the military was able to position its psychiatric casualty teams in-country and put into practice the lessons it had learned in both world wars. Although throughout the war the rate of psychiatric casualties was, on average, only slightly less than it had been in World War II, the reactions were generally less severe and more psychiatric casualties were returned to the fighting than in World War II.

World War II had shown that a major element in preventing battle shock was rooted in the strong peer attachments that members of combat groups formed with one another. Unit cohesion was regarded as the primary mechanism for keeping soldiers under stress functioning for acceptable periods of time. Unit cohesion provided support for the normal propensity of sane men not to want to be alone during times of stress. It supported as well the strong need to appear courageous or at least not fearful in the eyes of one's comrades. Despite all this, psychiatric casualty rates continued to be high as war became more destructive and lethal.

As important as unit cohesion was now seen to be, during the Korean War the military established a policy of individual replacement and rotation out of the combat zone rather than replacing and rotating whole units. As a consequence, once a soldier neared the end of his nine-month tour, he began to suffer from "short-timer's syndrome," a condition in which fear increases and combat performance declines. Often psychiatric symptoms would set in as the soldier was nearing the end of his tour of duty. Moreover, individual rotation and replacement made sustaining group cohesion more difficult. The soldier's attachment to his peers quickly shifted from his platoon to his buddy. Often when a buddy was killed the survivor felt alone and would become a psychiatric casualty. The military had learned the importance of group dynamics and attachments in sustaining sanity under stress, but failed to keep groups in place for long periods of time.

Once the war settled down into a stalemate, there was still the need to maintain large, fully armed forces constantly on the alert. Although clashes were few and far between, the soldier still found himself in a hostile environment deprived of many of the comforts of home. During periods of prolonged noncombat stress, psychiatric casualties began to occur once again at rates not appreciably lower than during combat. All the symptoms of nostalgia first seen among European armies in the sixteenth century and later among Civil War soldiers began to appear again. Nostalgia often manifested itself in secondary reactions such as frostbite, alcohol abuse, constant complaints of lower back pain, and general malaise. The experience of four centuries of soldiers under noncombat stress was repeated. Today, in 1987, large combat forces still remain on the Korean peninsula although they have not seen combat in over twenty years. Nonetheless, secondary symptoms of stress remain. In 1985, the combat force of 14,000 men stationed in Korea reported no fewer than 12,000 cases of venereal disease among its soldiers.

During the ten years of the Vietnam conflict the number of psychiatric cases evacuated out of the country was the lowest of any war in which America participated in this century. While there is no doubt that some of this was due to the presence of psychiatric teams to treat the problem in-country, there are other, more important reasons for this low rate. First, by any standard, Vietnam was a minor combat war. There were few large-scale engagements with the enemy and even these were of comparatively short duration, almost never lasting more than a few days. Second, the enemy possessed few weapons capable of inflicting heavy casualties. The Vietcong had little artillery and no capacity for air attack, which historically have produced large numbers of psychiatric casualties. Third, in Vietnam the war was a war of base camps. Typically, small American units would sally forth for a few days in search of the enemy, who usually refused to do battle. After a few days in the bush, American units would return to base camps where they were safe and surrounded by many of the comforts of home. Fourth, most combat actions were in ambushes, which, although terrifying, almost never lasted more than a minute or two at most. There was, in short, no prolonged combat stress for most American soldiers. Fifth, the American Army was so "tail-heavy"—that is, it had so many support troops in rear areas—that at the peak of American engagement in that war, 565,000 troops could muster only 88,000 combat troops to do battle. For most American soldiers in Vietnam, contact with the enemy was a rare thing indeed. Lastly, the short one-year tour of duty in-country joined with a number of other factors that relieved tension. Among these were the ready availability of prostitutes, bars, alcohol, music, phone calls home, and drugs.

During the periods of greatest combat action, most notably the Tet offensive of 1968 and the few set-piece battles that it produced (Hue, Saigon, Ban Me Thuot, and others), the rate of psychiatric casualties approached Korean and World War II levels. Most psychiatric casualties were of the nostalgia variety, now termed "disorders of loneliness." As the war drew to a close, the number of medical evacuations for these disorders skyrocketed. To be sure, many soldiers, far more than in any other war, carried away with them a number of psychiatric symptoms that did not come to the attention of military medical authorities in-country but which produced severe symptoms after the soldiers had returned to the United States. While the figures are unclear, estimates of soldiers suffering from Post-Traumatic Stress Disorder range from 500,000 to 1,500,000. If these figures are correct, Vietnam produced more psychiatric casualties than any other American war in its history.

The history of military psychiatry makes it clear that war tends to produce very large numbers of soldiers who suffer psychiatric collapse as a consequence of its horror. Moreover, for large numbers of soldiers, the strain of being in a military environment in a foreign land, even if there is no fighting or only a remote threat of combat, is too much for them to take. While their symptoms are not usually as dramatic as those found in soldiers exposed to direct combat, they are no less debilitating and of no less concern to the commander who is trying to maintain the fighting strength of his unit.

Moreover, it is clear that despite any number of attempts to prevent and deal with psychiatric casualties, the traditional methods so far attempted do not work very well. Even those treated successfully and returned to the line are likely once again to become psychiatric casualties. There seems no escape for most men.

All this suggests that psychiatric collapse in battle is the reaction of sane and normal men forced to adjust to insane and abnormal circumstances. Soldiers will continue to suffer psychiatric breakdown regardless of what military psychiatrists attempt to do about it. The causes of psychiatric collapse, it is worth repeating, have little to do with the soldier's character or his predisposition to weakness. Psychiatric breakdown is an inevitable by-product of war, as inevitable as the dead, the wounded, and the maimed. Far more important in understanding battle shock are the objective conditions of the battlefield that men must face. By any reasonable standard of comparison, until now those conditions have been mild compared to those which must be confronted by the soldier in modern war. That is why the traditional ways of dealing with the problem will no longer work.

Modern conventional war has become so lethal and so intense that only the already insane can endure it. As studies of World War II psychiatric casualties revealed, only those soldiers who were already aggressive psychopathic personalities before entering combat could remain mentally unbroken after thirty-five days of exposure to battle. The rest, sane men at the start, simply were driven to psychiatric collapse. The technology of modern war has reached a point where it will generate millions of psychiatric casualties while, at the same time, engendering conditions that makes treating these casualties almost impossible within the battle zone. Modern war will make the traditional means of dealing with the psychiatrically broken useless. The next war will confront man with the unsolvable problem of devising a solution to a problem of his own making.

Modern war requiring continuous combat will increase the degree of fatigue on the soldier to heretofore unknown levels. Physical fatigue—especially the lack of sleep—will increase the number of psychiatric casualties enormously. Other factors—high rates of indirect fire, night fighting, lack of food, constant stress, large numbers of casualties—will ensure that the number of psychiatric casualties will reach disastrous proportions. And the number of casualties will overburden the medical structure to the point of collapse.

The ability to treat psychiatric casualties will all but disappear. There will be no safe forward areas in which to treat soldiers debilitated by mental collapse. The technology of modern war has made such locations functionally obsolete. To take only one example, the ability of modern armies to locate aggregations of troops by the "infrared signatures" given off by groups of soldiers and their supporting equipment (trucks, generators, radios, etc.) makes forward-area facilities of any sort highly vulnerable to weapons ranging from rocket-assisted laser-guided artillery to attack helicopters. It will be next to impossible to maintain the geographic stability of medical stations near the front, because the front will be constantly shifting. When everyone is on the offensive, no unit, especially medical treatment stations, can remain in place without risking destruction.

Medical facilities far in the rear will be equally at risk as both sides engage in the "deep battle" for the precise purpose of destroying the enemy's supporting infrastructure. Each side will count heavily on the deep battle to paralyze the adversary. Moreover, in many instances, front-line strong points will be bypassed by attacking forces, who can inflict far more damage on the enemy's ability to continue the battle by disrupting his rear and can do so with far fewer losses than if front-line strong points are engaged. The merging of front-line and rear-area offensive and defensive forces into a giant swirling movement of destruction and death will make it impossible to maintain psychiatric facilities to treat casualties. Worse, a psychiatric casualty lucky enough to be evacuated to the rear might well find himself in a combat situation more intense than the front line. Alternatively, he may simply be killed along with the rest of the wounded huddled around a medical service point. Quite simply, there will no longer be any place for a casualty to be safe. Even the wounded will be at great risk.

Even if it were possible to stabilize psychiatric and medical treatment stations in safe areas in the rear, they would be too far to the rear to successfully treat the psychiatrically broken. Treatment must be provided in proximity to the battle. Experience has shown that if the patient is moved far to the rear, his symptoms tend to deepen and fixate, and his chances of recovering quickly enough to be returned to the battle are greatly reduced. Thus, evacuation in itself generates further psychiatric damage. Worse, once soldiers come to understand that medical evacuation is possible—indeed their only remote hope—more and more of them will begin to collapse. Any number of armies, from the Russians in 1904–5 to the Israelis in 1982, have witnessed the effect of the "evacuation syndrome" in increasing the rate of psychiatric breakdown.

Even if some way could be found to stabilize and protect front-line medical stations, the time required to restore the soldier to physiological and emotional health would be too great to make the return of the soldier to his unit practical. Many cases of psychiatric collapse respond quite rapidly to simple sleep, rest, and food. At the minimum, even these rudimentary therapies require twenty-four to forty-eight hours to work successfully. No one in his right mind would or could remain stationary on the modern battlefield for even this length of time. The need to move the patient at frequent intervals mitigates against rapid recovery.

Much is made of returning the soldier to his unit once he has recovered. The reason for this is that the soldier may have spent weeks or months with his comrades and his return strengthens the cohesion of the group. In addition, the return facilitates the soldier's own recovery. Experience in World War II and Korea shows clearly that soldiers who were not returned to their units were at greater risk of becoming psychiatric casualties again in a very short time. But in modern war, it is highly likely that it will be impossible to return soldiers to their units.

In the first place, a soldier's unit is likely to have moved on, for the mobility of the modern battlefield makes rapid movement the key to survival. A psychiatric casualty out of action for twenty-four hours would have little chance of finding his unit, let alone catching up with it. Moreover, there may simply be no point in finding one's old unit. It may have been decimated. During World War II, the Soviets made no attempt to return recovered wounded soldiers to their units for the simple reason that units engaged in battle often ceased to exist during the time it took a casualty to recover and return. Men in these units were replaced at such a rapid rate that a returning soldier was likely to find few of his old comrades alive. Instead, the Soviet Army collected casualties from aid stations and formed entirely new units and then committed them to battle. As expected, the number of soldiers who broke down again was very high. Even in so short a war as the Israeli invasion of Lebanon in 1982, IDF medical personnel found it very difficult to return recovered casualties to their own units. In most instances, recovered casualties couldn't find their units because they were moving so fast or the combat situation made it impossible to reach them.

Psychiatric casualties do not occur in a medical vacuum. Rather, they are part of the normal "casualty stream" comprised of thousands of physically wounded men. While neither the Soviets nor the Americans have been able to predict with any accuracy the level of casualties that will result from a modern conventional war, it can safely be assumed that it will reach over a hundred thousand within days of the outbreak of battle. The stream of casualties will reach enormous proportions and easily overwhelm the medical services. This will force medical personnel to resort to triage, which involves the separating of casualties into categories of seriousness in order to provide treatment first to those who have the best chance of survival. The most seriously wounded and incapacitated are treated last and often not treated at all. In triage situations physical casualties have priority of treatment and first claim on all medical resources, even though, paradoxically, psychiatric casualties are more likely to be able to return to action with minimal treatment. This situation, in which one must cruelly choose among what casualties to treat, was one in which the Soviet Army found itself many times during World War II. The Soviets always decided in favor of physical casualties.

Under these conditions, psychiatric casualties will build up around the few surviving medical servicing points. But there will be few medical personnel to care for them. It has already been pointed out that the medical structures of each side are severely deficient in manpower and would be unable to deal even with World War II-level surgical casualties.

The manpower available to treat psychiatric casualties is even more sorely deficient. In the Soviet Army, for example, there are no psychiatrists or psychiatric assistants located below army level. While the American Army intends to station psychiatrists and a complement of psychiatric assistants in every division, there are today only 213 psychiatrists in the entire Army and most of them are not stationed with combat divisions. This number of psychiatrists is less than the number stationed with U.S. forces in Europe during World War I.

These circumstances evoke a vision of thousands of psychiatric casualties clustered around the few surviving medical stations with no one to treat them. Groups of exhausted, blind, mute, and dazed men will be left unattended to roam about the battle area. These men, most of whom collapsed because they could not endure the horror at the front, now find themselves in a living hell in which the screams of the wounded and the sight of the dead and dying may be even more disturbing. If the medical station is attacked, hundreds of psychiatric casualties too stunned to defend themselves will be killed. If the medical station is warned of an impending attack, it will have to move rapidly and leave the mentally broken to shift for themselves. The vision of thousands of broken and helpless soldiers wandering aimlessly around the battlefield and in the rear areas is enough to give any soldier nightmares.

Conclusion

Even military medical professionals admit that the conditions on future conventional battlefields will make it virtually impossible for armies to deal even moderately well with the large numbers of broken soldiers which they expect to result from high-intensity combat. Certainly the more traditional methods of dealing with them, methods which were not very successful in previous wars, will not work. Modern war makes it likely that there will be no refuge in which to treat psychiatric casualties, few if any therapists to treat them, no time for adequate rest and recuperation, and no real possibility that soldiers will be able to return to their units. There will be thousands of mentally shattered men left to wander about in the battle zone until they are killed or maimed. Whatever glory war may once have afforded has rapidly disappeared, if, indeed, it ever existed at all.

5

The Chemical Soldier

In developing ever more destructive weapons to wage his wars man faces a technological paradox. War has become so destructive, lethal, and intense that it will generate rates of psychiatric casualties far in excess of what we have ever seen. At the same time, the nature of modern war will make it impossible to deal effectively with the explosion of psychiatric casualties that it will generate. But if man is to continue his fascination with the deadly business of war, this paradox cannot be allowed to stand for long. Either modern armies must find some way to deal with the problem of psychiatric debilitation or they must risk putting themselves out of business within days of going to war. If the old ways of dealing with it no longer work, then some new way must be found. The only alternative is to admit that war has become, in human terms, truly pointless.

Unable to successfully treat psychiatric breakdown in battle, armies have naturally turned their attention to trying to prevent it. In the past armies have sought to prevent psychiatric casualties by screening the manpower pool to identify individuals whom psychiatric tests define as prone to mental collapse, by reducing the time the soldier is exposed to combat, by increasing unit cohesion, and by providing realistic training. The most that can be said for these approaches is that they have worked only marginally in the past and will not work under the conditions of modern war.

In most cases psychiatric screening has failed to determine in advance the capacity of a soldier to endure combat stress. Indeed, most psychiatrists involved in the screening process for the U.S. military readily agree that the tests are highly unreliable and are poor predictors of behavior under fire. For the most part, they simply don't work.

Tests to determine emotional endurance are inevitably linked to the cultural values of the society administering them. Accordingly, predisposition to breakdown invariably becomes defined within the context of a nation's culture. There is no objective standard for determining endurance to stress any more than there is an objective standard for determining endurance to pain. Like pain, psychological stressors are best regarded as signals to the brain. It is the interpretation of these signals by the individual, not the signals themselves, which determines behavior. We know from experience with soldiers under stress that all sane men break down sooner or later. Only the already mentally disturbed seem capable of withstanding the stress of combat for long periods. Eventually, no doubt, someone will make the case for drafting only psychopaths, on the grounds that it will reduce psychiatric casualty rates. The disturbing fact is that an army of genuine aggressive psychopaths would have fewer psychiatric casualties!

Psychiatric screening for endurance to battle stress takes on a life of its own, often with disastrous results. The American experience with such screening in World War II resulted in the release from combat service of enough manpower to outfit fifty combat divisions. In fact, no one could really predict how these men would have performed under fire. They were excused from the fighting on the grounds that they had failed the test which had become the unquestioned standard. In World War I, there was no psychiatric screening until late in the war and there is absolutely no evidence that it reduced the psychiatric casualty rate. Indeed, the psychiatric casualty rate in World War II after screening was introduced was almost seven times that of World War I! The Soviet Union did not use screening at all in either war. Interestingly, the Soviet Army's rate of psychiatric casualties was about the same in both wars, about nine per thousand, and much below that suffered by the U.S. Army in World War II. If modern armies are going to prevent psychiatric casualties, they are certainly going to have to find another method.

Armies have also attempted to prevent psychiatric casualties by reducing the amount of time soldiers are exposed to combat. In Korea and Vietnam soldiers were exposed to the battle environment for limited combat tours of nine months and twelve months, respectively. The Israelis make much of telling their troops that their exposure to battle will, in the normal course, be only for a comparatively short while. In Lebanon, Israeli combat soldiers were often rotated out of the battle on a weekly basis. The idea behind such rotation is an old one. Throughout history actual combat in wars was usually confined to a single day. Even when it lasted longer, which was rare, nightfall provided a significant respite from stress and time to recoup. In World War I, the average amount of time a combat battalion actually spent on the line was about eight days. After that, it was rotated behind the line for a week or so while another battalion took its place.

Limiting exposure to battle to reduce combat stress has some validity. Unfortunately, the nature of modern war will make it impossible to rotate units out of battle on a regular basis. A major characteristic of modern war is continual engagement on the offensive. It is hard to imagine a commander on the attack breaking off the fight in order to rotate troops. It is even harder to imagine that a unit under attack will be given sufficient respite to replace its losses. The idea, after all, once one has paid the price of inflicting high casualties in the initial phases of an attack, is to take maximum advantage of the defender's weakened position and drive the attack home until the defender collapses. In Soviet doctrine, a unit engaged in an attack which suffers heavy casualties is not pulled from the line. Rather, weak spots are reinforced with new units. The remnants of the first unit are transferred to the reinforcing unit and are expected to continue the attack. Only by unrelenting attack can a breakthrough be fully exploited. It was common practice in World War II for Soviet units engaged in the attack to fight down to 25 percent strength, thus routinely absorbing 75 percent casualties!

Even if it were possible to pull units out of the line for rest and replenishment, there is no guarantee at all that they would not be attacked in the rear area under a deep-battle attack by the enemy. Equally important, the dynamics of psychiatric collapse indicate clearly that anxiety in the soldier can continue for days before and after a battle. This anxiety can easily result in psychiatric collapse before the battle. In World War II, almost 200,000 U.S. fighting men were psychiatrically debilitated even before their units left the United States. These men simply could not deal with the thought of war, never mind participation in combat. Accordingly, removing men from the fight for a period of a few days will inevitably result in large numbers of them developing psychiatric symptoms as a defense against having to go back.

In World War II American soldiers who had been given leave repeatedly collapsed when told they were being returned to the front. Bomber pilots who had flown several missions and were back at their bases often broke down when told they had to fly again in a few days. The night before a mission Army Air Force medical stations were routinely full of pilots manifesting psychiatric symptoms. In the early days of the war a common practice was to force them into their aircraft at pistol point. Man seems to be the only animal capable of being traumatized by what *might* happen. The less blessed members of the animal community restrict their worrying to what *is* happening to them. Perhaps that is why we attribute mental illness only to human beings.

To some the answer to preventing psychiatric collapse rests in man's strong social instincts and attachments. It is well known that men in combat groups bond strongly to one another. In military writings on unit cohesion, one consistently finds the assertion that the bonds combat soldiers form with one another are stronger than the bonds most men have with their wives and, indeed, this seems at times to be true. Nor is it uncommon for military writers to stress that a good commander must "love his troops" in order to command. According to military lore, officers must lead from the front—however impractical that may be in combat—and that officers may eat only after their troops have been fed. Young officers in every army are taught that an officer must never expect his men to endure hardships and risks that he is not himself prepared to endure. In the words of one well-known military analyst and combat officer, "a man who cannot love cannot command."[1]

There is no doubt that strong unit cohesion offers some protection against psychiatric breakdown. It also is a stimulus to acts of unusual bravery. Audie Murphy, the most decorated soldier on the American side in World War II, was once asked what moved him to single-handedly take on a German infantry company and kill all the men in it. His response was simply that "they were killing my friends." It is also true that elite units tend to have about a third fewer psychiatric casualties than non-elite units, suggesting that strong ties to one's comrades do indeed help in warding off the pressure of stress.

But if cohesion helps it certainly is no guarantee. Also, it is very doubtful that cohesion can be maintained in a modern war. Most studies on cohesion use as a standard the professional, highly trained regiments of the British and German armies of the past. In those units all men were volunteers, served long periods of time together, deployed as units, and lived together. For most armies of the world these conditions are no longer possible. In the first place, no nation could sustain sufficiently large numbers of standing units of professionals without going bankrupt. As a consequence, most modern armies are either conscript armies (Germany, the Soviet Union, France) or small professional armies of volunteers (Britain, the United States, Canada) that will require conscript reinforcements once the shooting starts. Moreover, once battle begins, whatever cohesion that existed will last only a few days, until the unit suffers its share of casualties. Then the combat units (platoons, companies, battalions, etc.) can only be sustained by a constant stream of conscript replacements inserted into the units as individual "fillers." The men in these units, quite naturally, will have had almost no time to train together and will hardly know one another. Within a few days the highly cohesive peacetime standing regiments will have been decimated and their personnel replaced at least twice. While unit cohesion may help somewhat in warding off psychiatric collapse, future wars will not be fought by highly disciplined "bands of brothers" with a long shared experience. Rather, they will be fought by a constantly changing stream of green troops who are strangers to one another. Cohesion may help, but the conditions of modern war make it impossible to sustain it for very long. Modern war will truly be, as the American Army has called it, a "come as you are" war.

Finally, in the past psychiatric collapse has been reduced by realistic training. While there are any number of fears a man brings with him to battle, among the most disturbing is fear of the unexpected. Soldiers are supposed to be trained under realistic conditions to acquaint them with the "real" battlefield so that they are not shocked when committed to the fighting. In the past it was possible to train troops to deal with the realistic conditions that they would find on the battlefield. Today, it is no longer possible.

Modern war is so lethal and so intense that there is no feasible way of training troops for what to expect. To be sure, it is possible, and vital, for troops to learn certain procedures and skills without which they would surely become easy victims. But one cannot, as the Soviets say, "steel the will" of the soldier for actual combat without committing him to it. The Soviet Army, which has the most extensive theory and practice in techniques for conditioning the soldier to function on the battlefield, also recognizes that, for the most part, the conditioning will not be effective when the shooting starts. Accordingly, the Soviet soldier is also told that there are spies in his ranks to report and deal with any errant behavior under fire and that he will be summarily shot if he fails to perform. Lest there be any doubt, the Soviets point out that in World War II no fewer than 250 general officers were shot for cowardice.[2] Battlefield motivation in the Soviet Army is instilled mostly by fear: a soldier who breaks under fire and fails to perform will be shot.

The inescapable fact, however, is that the circumstances of modern war will be so different that there is no longer any reasonable expectation that the traditional ways of preventing psychiatric collapse can work. The conditions of today's battlefield leave the soldier almost defenseless against the stress which it inflicts upon him. The result will inevitably be mental breakdown among very large numbers of combatants.

No government can allow such a state of affairs to persist for very long without having to admit that its huge expenditures for weapons and large standing military forces have no practical point except to provide jobs and careers. Worse, for governments to concede that armies will only succeed in generating large numbers of dead, wounded, maimed, and men made mad is to concede that conventional war will fail to produce clear-cut winners and losers. Both sides will absorb such high numbers of casualties as to make all victories Pyrrhic.

Military technology abhors a vacuum and there is no doubt that a vacuum exists between what the soldier is expected to do in modern war and what he can realistically be expected to do. Either some way must be found to prevent psychiatric collapse under fire or modern war will remain no less a mutual military suicide pact than nuclear war, with the single saving grace that most of its victims will be soldiers instead of the men, women, and children who are the present hostages to nuclear weapons. It should come as no surprise that the military establishments of the world are even now involved in developing a chemical solution to the problem.

The Chemical Soldier

The idea of trying to control soldiers' fears through chemical means is very old, although the degree of success has been low. For millennia commanders recognized that the main enemy on the battlefield was fear. Far more battles were won or lost because one side's troops had their spirit broken than through military genius or the rate of actual killing. Very commonly, the serious killing commenced only after one side broke, allowing the winners to pursue the vanquished and to slaughter them. Far more battles have been lost to fear than to the "push of the pike."

The first attempt we know of to control soldiers' fears by chemical means came two thousand years before the rise of Rome, and it remains among the most interesting examples of such attempts. Ancient tribes living on the steppes of central Russia apparently used chemical means to reduce fear and increase the fighting power of their warriors. These chemicals seem to have approached the effectiveness of attempts being made by modern armies. The Koyak and Wiros tribes perfected a drug made from the *Amanita muscaria* mushroom, a red-speckled cousin of the deadly "Angel of Death."[3]

The shamans of the tribes discovered that *A. muscaria* contained a powerful compound which, when consumed, had a powerful analgesic effect on the body, rendering it highly resistant to pain. It was probably originally used in religious ceremonies, but it was not long before a more pragmatic military use was found, to increase the ability of warriors to do battle. The shamans also learned that when a warrior urinated after eating the mushroom, the potency of the drug in his urine was many times greater than before. Warriors would then store the urine and drink it on the eve of battle. After a while they hit on the idea of feeding the mushroom to reindeer and gathering their urine. Apparently, the compound passed almost unmetabolized through the reindeer's kidneys, which provided a more efficient metabolic filter, thus increasing the potency of the drug. In this way the early shamans were able to produce a powerful chemical compound that was of great value.

The effect on the fighting capability of the warriors was dramatic. Apparently, men who took the drug became almost totally immune to pain and at the same time became capable of great feats of physical strength and endurance. Warriors were able to carry heavy loads great distances and had greater physical strength and stamina in battle. What is most interesting is that the drug apparently did not reduce the mental awareness of the soldiers and, like a natural amphetamine, might well have enhanced it for a short period of time. Equally important, the soldiers were able to sleep normally.

While there is no evidence on how long the drug's effects lasted, it is clear from history that the Koyaks and Wiros became very successful military societies whose warriors were feared for their brutality and endurance in battle. Indeed, there is some evidence that their military culture may have spread as far east as India, where some religious cults today continue to produce and consume a similar extract made from *Amanita muscaria*.

Drug use in battle was practiced throughout military history. In the thirteenth century the Crusaders fought a band of Moslem warriors known as "hashshashin," so called because they used hashish prior to battle to reduce fear and control pain. The modern English word "assassin" is derived from the "hashshashin" who made a practice of sneaking up on their enemy and killing them in the fashion of modern-day Gurkhas. In the sixteenth century the Spanish conquistador Juan Pizarro encountered Inca warriors who increased their endurance and resistance to fear and pain by chewing on the coca leaf, from which cocaine is derived.

In the British Army soldiers have traditionally been given a double jigger of rum to steel their nerves before battle. In World Wars I and II, the Russian Army, in addition to providing vodka, administered a number of chemicals derived from plants to improve the fighting ability of their soldiers. Such natural drugs as valerian, a mild but effective tranquilizer, were given to soldiers to calm them. Present-day Soviet parachutist manuals recommend giving a soldier caffeine in tea or coffee to "open the pathways to the brain" before committing him to battle. Caffeine, of course, is a stimulant that increases awareness. During the Vietnam War, American soldiers often used marijuana, alcohol, or hard drugs like heroin, despite official regulations to the contrary, to help them endure battle stress and the conditions of military life.

The chemical solution to overcoming fear and increasing battle performance has a long history. But what modern armies have in mind far surpasses anything that might have been used in the past. Biology and chemistry have combined to produce the modern science of biochemistry, which seeks to understand and reduce human behavior to chemical reactions at the molecular level in the body and the brain. Man's new understanding of molecular bonding has brought into existence a wide range of chemical compounds that do not exist in nature. They are products of man's ingenuity. Armed with this new knowledge, the military research medical establishments of the world have set for themselves the task of abolishing fear in the soldier and making him a more efficient killing machine.

Anxiety is central to man's ability to survive as a species. It provides him with a mechanism to protect himself from mortal danger. Any animal that cannot feel anxiety will be unable to detect dangers which threaten its existence. All animals, including man, are equipped by nature with anxiety-producing mechanisms to warn of impending dangers.

Anxiety is vital for survival. Once danger is detected, anxiety prepares the mind and body to deal with the danger. Without anxiety man would easily be destroyed in much greater numbers, which, in turn, would limit his reproduction rate, which, in the end, would threaten the perpetuation of the species. From a purely biological and evolutionary perspective, anxiety serves the same ends in all animals, including man.

The onset of anxiety prepares the mind and body to engage in "flight or fight." Both responses are equally functional insofar as they deal with the threat to life. Anxiety triggers a reaction in the limbic region of the brain, which sends chemical signals to the body and the rest of the brain. In response to these signals the body's blood pressure, heart rate, respiration rate, and muscular capacity all increase. These responses make the body a more efficient fighting machine by increasing its strength, endurance, and resistance to pain. This is why soldiers placed under stress are capable of great feats of strength and endurance. Men have been known to carry their wounded buddies more than a mile under enemy fire or, in just as many cases, flee across very rough terrain without difficulty. For a short time the body reaches peak physical efficiency to deal with threats to its existence.

At the same time a series of chemicals called neurotransmitters are released within the brain which facilitate the ability of the brain's nerve synapses to transmit impulses along its nerve pathways. These neurotransmitters increase the brain's ability to function, especially by increasing its state of mental awareness. Under stress, these neurotransmitters make it possible for mental functions to become extremely acute, matching the body's increase in physiological awareness. Not only do the soldier's senses of smell, sight, and hearing become more acute, but the ability of the brain to interpret and assign meaning to these signals increases greatly. At this point, the whole animal mechanism is ready to do combat and, if necessary, sustain injury and endure pain.

Under conditions of short-lived fear this state of increased readiness is functional to survival and it can be sustained for hours. Usually, once the threat has been reduced or has disappeared, the body and brain return to normal levels of physiological readiness. This reduction in anxiety is also controlled by the brain. If anxiety persists for too long, however, it is possible for the physiological effects of stress—increased blood pressure, heart rate, respiration, etc.—to become fixed at very high levels which cannot easily be reduced by the natural control mechanisms of the body and brain. In these instances, the soldier must be given medication or long periods of rest away from danger to return his body and mind to their normal state.

But the battlefield puts tremendous levels of stress on the soldier even when he is not directly engaged in fighting. The mind can readily generate anxiety over conditions which it expects to meet as well as over those it must deal with directly. The levels of stress under which soldiers must function are usually much higher than those found under normal circumstances. Under conditions of sustained high stress the neurotransmitters of the brain can run out of control. The chemical neurotransmitters are produced in greater quantities than the brain and nerve pathways can handle. A runaway series of chemical reactions is triggered by and within the brain.

When this occurs, the soldier becomes a candidate for rapid psychiatric collapse and he may suffer the onset of severe neurosis or rapid psychosis. A number of conditions may arise in the brain in consonance with this condition. The normally circular pattern of production and reduction of certain neurotransmitters may break down in such a way that the brain is unable to control its own chemical functions. In other instances, the supply of a critical chemical compound may be entirely depleted, which may, in turn, interfere with the ability of the brain to sustain a complex chemical reaction cycle. In still other instances, the receptors of the brain's nerve synapses may be chemically blocked. Finally, as a consequence of any or all of these conditions, the ability of the brain to produce other important neurotransmitters may cease altogether. Under any of these conditions a state of complete exhaustion may result in which the soldier becomes totally unable to function mentally.

The effects on the soldier are traumatic. Once the chemical reactions in the brain are disturbed as a consequence of prolonged and severe anxiety the soldier may find it impossible to sleep. When he does fall asleep he may find it almost impossible to wake up or to reach a state of full consciousness. His mental abilities fall off rapidly and he has great difficulty comprehending even the simplest instructions. His memory, especially his short-term memory, declines greatly. The soldier becomes unable to process information and make decisions regarding even his own safety. His mental functions simply won't work normally since the brain can no longer chemically sustain a normal level of mental awareness. Thus, the soldier is placed at risk of total mental collapse. The effects of this process can take days to emerge or, as is very common, can occur in a matter of hours or even minutes.

If the military is to prevent the onset of anxiety as a

prophylactic for psychiatric collapse, the key is to somehow prevent the chemical reactions in the body and brain from becoming so acute that they produce a mental collapse. There are already a number of drugs that can be used to prevent or control anxiety. Some of the more common ones are Librium, Elavil, and Valium. All of these drugs present major problems when used by soldiers to reduce the effects of battle stress. All of them control the onset of anxiety by preventing the brain from producing its normal level of certain neurotransmitters. Anxiety is reduced, but there is an accompanying and often greater reduction in the ability of the brain to process information and think quickly. A soldier who cannot think clearly and quickly is more likely to become a casualty. Another problem is that these drugs interfere with normal sleep, often producing nightmares or feelings of increased fatigue. Their effects last only a short time, and when they wear off, the soldier is often plunged more deeply into anxiety. In short, the price of purchasing a decrease in anxiety with the drugs we have is to dull the mental abilities of the soldier, a condition that is actually more dangerous to his survival.

The problem to be solved is to find a chemical compound that will prevent or reduce anxiety while allowing the soldier to retain his normal levels of acute mental awareness. Such a compound would have to affect the chemical processes in the brain which govern the reactions to anxiety without depleting the normal function of the nerve synapses responsible for mental activity. In scientific terminology, the search is for a "nondepleting neurotrop." A neurotrop is a chemical compound that works directly on the transmitters and receptors of the brain's nerve pathways.

The search for such a chemical is already underway in the military research laboratories of the major armies of the world. Both the U.S. military and the Soviets have initiated programs in the last five years to develop such a drug; the details of the American program remain classified. The search has taken on increased urgency in light of the belated recognition that modern war is so stressful that it will break most normal men within a matter of days if not hours. U.S. Army estimates, produced from computer models, predict that psychiatric casualties will account for 40 to 50 percent of the casualties in a modern conventional war. It is likely that the next revolution in military power will occur, not in weapons technology, but in chemistry that will make it possible for soldiers to endure the conditions of modern war brought about by the new weapons. The U.S. military has already developed at least three prototypes that show great "promise." One of these drugs may be a variant of busbirone. If the search is successful, and it almost inevitably will be, the relationship between soldiers and their battle environment will be transformed forever. And there will be no going back.

If the military establishments of the United States and the Soviet Union succeed in developing a chemical compound that will prevent the onset of anxiety while allowing the soldier to remain mentally alert, sleep normally, and process information under stress, the nature of war, already too horrible to seriously contemplate, will become even more horrible. In solving one problem the military establishments will create even greater problems, for they will change man's psychic nature. If they succeed, they will have finally done what man has been incapable of doing since he first emerged from the primal mud: they will have banished the fear of death and with it will go man's humanity and his soul.

A truly effective anxiety-controlling drug will make paralyzing fear an anachronism. Soldiers will be unable to develop deep fears for their lives or their own safety. To be sure, there will remain an intellectual commitment to staying alive, but the physiological support mechanisms which make the fear of death real and functional on the battlefield will simply not engage. No longer will anxiety trigger the body's endocrine system to raise the pulse rate, raise body temperature, dilate the pupils, and stimulate respiration. Nor will the muscles spring to life at the thought of fear which sends adrenaline racing through the bloodstream. The fear of death may remain in the conscious mind, but there will be no physiological or emotional support to make the fear real. Men may still *know* fear; but they will be unable to *feel* fear in an emotional sense. The chemical soldier will be a reality and the reality will be a chemically created monster.

Abolishing fear on the battlefield will change the nature of both man and war, for fear has a very real influence on men in battle. Its most obvious effect is that it reduces the killing power of the soldier. Frightened soldiers don't kill very well and, in the past, this has made the level of war manageable in human terms. It is worth recalling that in World War II only 15 percent of the soldiers engaged in combat ever fired their weapons. This, of course, kept the casualties down. But if chemical preventives for fear succeed in controlling anxiety in only 75 percent of the soldiers, 75 percent of the combat soldiers on the battlefield will be sufficiently mentally alert to kill other soldiers, an increase in the killing capability of 400 percent at the very minimum! And since the killing power of weaponry has increased by a factor of at least ten since World War II, the increase in the destructiveness and intensity of war in the future will be enormous. And it will be achieved by simply increasing the "human potential" of the combat soldier. To be sure, a chemical preventive will reduce the rate of psychiatric casualties, but it will purchase this reduction at the price of exponentially increasing the number of dead and wounded.

Not only will more soldiers be able to kill, but they will be able to kill far more efficiently. Men suffering physiological and emotional stress reactions have great difficulty processing information, aiming weapons, and operating equipment, all vital tasks in the killing business. At present, one of the advantages of high-tech weaponry is that soldiers can use it easily, for it simplifies many of the physical and mental operations. With the soldiers' stress reactions chemically under control, they will be able to operate their killing machines with much greater efficiency for much longer periods. The result, not unexpectedly, will be a much greater degree of lethality.

In a war of chemical soldiers, military units, once engaged, will scarcely be able to disengage. In earlier battles one side or the other simply absorbed as much death as it could until its spirit broke, at which point it either withdrew or surrendered. In either case battle had its limits and the defeated remnants at least survived. Fear put real limits on the ability of units to attack or defend and, in most cases, it was this element which permitted victory or defeat. The chemical soldier will fight without fear to limit his ability to kill. The continuous offensive will be matched by the continuous defensive. Battles once joined will proceed until one side has been entirely killed or wounded. Without fear, battles will be fought to the death as a matter of routine because there will no longer be any reason to stop them.

Without psychiatric collapse and fear to force defenders to surrender when all is lost, units will resist to the last man. This will force the attackers, including the officers, to kill them all in a sterile exercise of military slaughter. It will be battle without prisoners. The defenders will be unable to surrender and the attackers will be unable to offer it, for the basis of surrender, the fear of death, will no longer be present in the chemically bemused minds of the combatants. In past wars large numbers of potential dead men escaped by surrendering and becoming prisoners. Now the soldier will no longer even be afforded that luxury. He will be expected to fight to the death as the full measure of military efficiency.

In the world of chemical combat soldiers and officers there will be no military ethos. It will be replaced by technical proficiency measured by the body count. For four thousand years military ethos traditionally has set limits on killing by requiring the victor to place himself as a fellow human being in the place of the vanquished. Soldiers have always had codes of ethics which guided their treatment of the soldiers against whom they fought. It was this empathy that led armies in the past to limit the killing. Without fear there is no basis for empathy or sympathy for the loser. Military ethos will be replaced by efficiency and the killing will go on.

The West's sense of traditional military ethos is derived from the Greek military experience, which placed human qualities over technical ones even to the point of refusing to adopt more efficient military technologies on the grounds that they were inhuman and dishonorable. For the Greeks, war remained a bloody but nonetheless human endeavor. It was men and their actions that made war tolerable, not the mere exercise of military technique. The ends for which wars were fought and the manner in which they were fought were central to a moral view of war. It was the human dimension of war, the ability of the human being to endure in a terrible environment and to limit the killing, that gave a soldier his human and ethical worth.

For the chemical soldier military virtues will have no meaning and no function. Qualities such as courage, bravery, endurance, and sacrifice have meaning only in human terms. They indicate conditions in which men triumph over normal fear. Heroes are those who can endure and control fear beyond the limits expected of normally sane men. Brave men are those who conquer fear. Sacrifice for one's comrades can only have meaning when one fears death and accepts it because it will prevent others from dying or will permit an idea to live. If fear is eliminated from the soldier through chemical means, there will be nothing over which he can triumph. The standards of normal men will be eroded and will disappear. Men will be dehumanized and will no longer die for anything that is meaningful in truly human terms. They will just die. The military virtues—courage, heroism, endurance, bravery, and sacrifice—will be replaced in war by probability tables that measure the technical efficiency of "human" performance. And the standard of performance will be the body count.

In a real sense, the advent of the chemical soldier will change not only the nature and intensity of warfare but the psychological nature of man himself. It will change the very basis of human emotion and action as we have always known it. A chemical compound that prevents the onset of anxiety while leaving the individual mentally alert will produce a new kind of human being, a human being who would retain the cognitive elements of his emotions but would be unable to feel emotion. The basis of all human emotion is anxiety, and without this physiological basis those elements of mental operation that give the cognitive element true meaning in human terms would no longer be present in the mental processes of the soldier. Emotions are rooted in anxiety and anxiety would disappear for as long as the chemical compound worked on the neurotransmitters of the brain. The interaction between the cognitive and the physiological aspects of emotion, both vitally necessary for emotions to exist, would disappear. And along with it what we know as the soul would be destroyed.

We would be left with a genuine sociopathic personality induced and sustained by chemical means. A sociopathic personality is one who clearly *knows* what he is doing to another person but cannot *feel* or appreciate in an emotional sense the consequences of his actions. Although sociopathic personalities are above average in intelligence, they often cannot prevent themselves from acting even though they know (but cannot truly feel) what the consequences of their actions might be. Sociopaths are unable to display loyalty to others, are grossly selfish, are unable to feel guilt or remorse or appreciate the consequences of their actions. They are given to extreme risk taking and generally lack the normal characteristics which we commonly associate with conscience. The sociopath functions only on the cognitive plane of his emotions. That is why true sociopaths cannot empathize or sympathize with those who may be hurt by their actions. To be sure, they know cognitively that they have inflicted pain but they cannot generate a genuine emotional response to this fact. The chemical soldier will be a true sociopath.

Richard Hechtl, who has spent fifteen years working with sociopathic personalities, says that it appears as if significant changes have occurred in the chemical biology of the sociopath's brain operations. In Hechtl's words, "their capacity to respond normally to anxiety-provoking stimuli has been diminished as to suggest an absence or paucity of appropriate neurotransmitters."[4] The sociopathic personality suffers from a chemical interruption in the brain which prohibits the nerve pathways from chemically transmitting the physiological aspects of emotion to the brain. The physiological elements of anxiety reactions are blocked by a chemical debilitation from entering into the mental processes. The sociopathic personality operates in the realm of his emotions on only one cylinder, the cognitive or purely intellectual one. He remains deficient in his ability to experience emotional responses within a human context. It is precisely these conditions which will be produced in the chemical soldier.

The real horror lurking behind the attempt to use chemical means for preventing psychiatric collapse in battle is that in order for a soldier to be able to function in the environment of modern war he must be psychically reconstituted to become what we have traditionally defined as mentally ill! He must be chemically made over to become a sociopathic personality in the clinical sense of the term. The soldier must be made abnormal in order to behave "normally" on the battlefield. If he is to function efficiently, he must first be made insane.

Psychiatric collapse under fire, it bears repeating, is not the reaction of the weak or the cowardly. Rather, it is the reaction of the normally sane to an insane environment. As the data from World War II demonstrate, only the clinically ill—aggressive psychopathic personalities—remain immune to psychiatric collapse. The chemical solution will make it possible for the sane soldier to survive psychically in an insane environment only by making him as clinically insane as the environment in which he is expected to function!

Under these circumstances, abnormality becomes normality and the psychic nature of man along with clinical definitions of sanity are altered forever. The paradox is that in order for the soldier to survive he must first be emotionally destroyed. And with this destruction, the human dimensions of war—bravery, sacrifice, endurance, heroism—disappear too.

Conclusion

On the battlefields of the future we will witness a true clash of ignorant armies, armies ignorant of their own emotions and even of the reasons for which they fight. Soldiers on all sides will be reduced to fearless chemical automatons who fight simply because they can do nothing else and because nothing else any longer "rationally" matters. The soldier will become no more than one more death-inflicting combat machine—like tanks, missiles, and guns—to be used by commanders in much the same way. There will no longer be any way to make the loss of men in battle meaningful in human terms. Their loss will make even less sense to their mothers, wives, brothers, and children, who, safely removed from the chemically induced haze, will retain their sense of emotional balance, human judgment, and moral horror. For them, the death of their loved ones will make no sense at all. Life-and-death decisions, especially for commanders who commit their men to action, will become mere exercises in technical expertise totally devoid of human content. Men will fight and die because they fight and die. Nothing more.

Even those who fight and survive will have precious little to show for it in human terms. Battle will no longer be a fearful or exciting experience. It will be an experience devoid of human emotion and meaning, akin to that felt by a strongly tranquilized individual carelessly driving an automobile on a rain-swept winding road at high speed. He recognizes the danger intellectually, but he continues his course because the danger has no genuine emotional meaning and his behavior is unaffected.

Under these conditions soldiers will be able to stay "sane." They will "know" that their comrades have been killed, but it will not affect them; they will "know" that they have destroyed other men, but it will not matter; they will "know" that their actions killed innocent civilians, but they will not feel it; and they will "know" when they are about to meet their own ends, but it will not matter much. There will be no fear. The soldier will lack the capacity for emotional response and be left without human standards to measure or limit his actions. Amid the death, pain, and horror, the chemical soldier will simply fight on.

Nor is there any good reason to think that once it becomes possible to banish fear in the soldier the search for a more efficient killer will stop. Once the chemical genie is out of the bottle, the full range of human mental and physical actions become targets for chemical control. The search to improve the military potential of the human being will move on to press the very limits of humanity itself. Consider, for example, what can be gained in human potential on the battlefield if, once fear is banished, chemical means are found to increase the aggressiveness of the individual soldier. Today it is already possible by chemical or electric stimulation to increase the aggression levels of human beings by stimulating the amygdala, a section of the brain known to control aggression and rage. Such "human potential engineering" is already a partial reality and the necessary technical knowledge increases every day. Faceless, well-meaning military medical researchers press the limits of their discipline with little or no regard for the consequences. We may be rushing headlong into a long, dark chemical night from which there will be no return. The paradox is that it is necessary to enslave the emotions as the means of producing soldiers who can defend a nation's freedoms.

6

No More War

Even devout military metaphysicians recognize that nuclear war has become an immoral horror, nothing short of suicide. But military thinkers and planners continue to console themselves with the belief that conventional war is still an acceptable substitute and, consequently, have continued to increase weapons technology without any significant hindrances from either the American people or their political leaders. It is difficult to find a single major conventional weapons system that has not been approved by Congress in the last decade. Debate over what weapons to build has been limited to nuclear weapons. Approval for conventional weaponry has been granted almost without hesitation, perhaps in the belief that if the military is given more conventional weapons to play with they will be more reasonable on the issue of nuclear arms. The result has been to develop a conventional arsenal whose effectiveness begins to approach that of nuclear weapons.

Both the Soviet and the American military have developed conventional weapons that make those used in World War II pale by comparison. The explosive capacity of most modern weapons exceeds that of World War II weapons by at least five times. Rates of fire have increased by almost ten times. Accuracy has increased by twenty times and the ability to detect enemy targets has increased several hundred percent. On top of all this has been the introduction of weapons systems undreamed of in 1945. The overall result is that the ability of modern armies to deliver a combat punch has increased by at least 600 percent since the end of World War II. Military technology has reached a point where "conventional weapons have unconventional effects." In both conventional war and nuclear war, combatants can no longer be reasonably expected to survive.

Confronting the real consequences of conventional war drives men mad in droves. War has reached the point where most human beings can no longer remain sane long enough to produce any military outcome except collective death and insanity. Exposure to modern war crushes the fragile mental defenses with which man protects himself against insanity. Man's profound belief that he can overcome danger—that he will survive, that his actions influence what happens to him, and that someone, even God, will help him get through the horror—collapses within days, often hours, of being exposed to the terrible realities of the battlefield. And with them go the last anchors of man's sanity. Insanity provides at least some escape, however twisted and bizarre.

Faced with a choice between death and insanity, most civilians engage in denial. Unable to face the realities of war, most of us refuse to think about it, choosing to leave military technology and fighting to the experts. Since even the experts have a limited capacity to face the truth, they, too, deny reality on the grounds that they are only doing their jobs. As small cogs in a huge weapons machine, they would argue, it is hardly fair to hold them responsible for the consequences of the larger military system. If anyone is at fault it is the system itself. So the game goes on.

For most Americans war is merely theater. It is, perhaps, understandable that a people who have barely been scratched by war should be tolerant of it and, to a great extent, almost mesmerized by it. Perhaps in a nation where television programs have become, for many, the reality against which to assess their own feelings about war, this is inevitable. Yet anyone who has ever been a soldier understands that war has always been theater. Most young men willingly join or accept conscription into the military establishments of their countries. It is no accident that after the American air strike against Libya in 1986 volunteers for the military increased. Having witnessed wars mostly in theaters or on television screens, most of us accept the film as reality.

War has always had a romantic attraction and it has always exercised a particularly strong influence over the young men who fight it. Many a young soldier has visions of glory, of women who will love him for serving his country, of being tested against himself, of showing his father, his older brother, or his peers that he is a man, and of proving to the women who rejected him what fools they were. It is the images of war in the minds of the young that are so compelling. In truth, the realities have never been squarely faced by the recruit. And by the time the shooting starts, it is too late to escape.

In the past, wars were tolerable enough to allow some romantic notions to survive. Indeed, to many soldiers a slight wound was the ultimate symbol that he had faced the challenge and triumphed. And to many an old soldier, a vital part of having survived was the opportunity to tell the younger generation how bravely he fought and how fearless he was. Having survived a war provided one with something to be proud of as the years stole one's youth and crushed one's illusions. Today, the romance and glory of war persist as realities when they are but myths.

In order to tolerate the killing, men have always convinced themselves that the enemy was different, that he did not have a family, or that he was inferior in any number of ways. In earlier times, tribes took names which meant "man" or "human being," thus automatically defining those outside the tribe as something less than men. This made killing them easier. Today, we use ethnic, political, or racial epithets—Jap, gook, slope, dink, Commie—which serve the same dehumanizing purpose. These mental gymnastics, called intraspeciation by psychologists, allow us to kill with impunity because the enemy is "not like us." One can only marvel at the statements of today's nuclear metaphysicians who work in the Pentagon's think tanks designing nuclear strike strategies. When confronted by the fact that the Russians lost twenty million people in World War II and that their country was devastated, they respond that precisely because of those past losses the Russians do not fear war as much as other peoples. And because the Soviets once endured such terrible losses, the only way to make any nuclear strategy truly credible is to ensure that they know that future losses would be even greater! The mind game goes on regardless of realities.

Men dehumanize the enemy as the only way to justify their own horrible acts. Otherwise, it would be impossible to remove the blood from the soldier's hands. Once the battlefield expunges the myths which propelled the soldier to do battle, he must deal with the realities of death and destruction. And the only way to cope with them and remain sane is to dehumanize the enemy. To recognize him as human is to squarely face what one has done. And that is no easy task; for some it is impossible.

Societies have always recognized that war changes men, that they are not the same after they return. That is why primitive societies often required soldiers to perform purification rites before allowing them to rejoin their communities. These rites often involved washing or other forms of ceremonial cleansing. Psychologically, these rituals provided soldiers with a way of ridding themselves of stress and the terrible guilt that always accompanies the sane after war. It was also a way of treating guilt by providing a mechanism through which fighting men could decompress and relive their terror without feeling weak or exposed. Finally, it was a way of telling the soldier that what he did was right and that the community for which he fought was grateful and that, above all, his community of sane and normal men welcomed him back.

Modern armies have similar mechanisms of purification. In World War II soldiers en route home often spent days together on troopships. Among themselves, the warriors could relive their feelings, express grief for lost comrades, tell each other about their fears, and, above all, receive the support of their fellow soldiers. They were provided with a sounding board for their own sanity. Upon reaching home, soldiers were often honored with parades or other civic tributes. They received the respect of their communities as stories of their experiences were told to children and relatives by proud parents and wives. All of this served the same cleansing purpose as the rituals of the past.

When soldiers are denied these rituals they often tend to become emotionally disturbed. Unable to purge their guilt or be reassured that what they did was right, they turn their emotions inward. The effect can be devastating. Soldiers returning from the Vietnam War were victims of this kind of neglect. There were no long troopship voyages where they could confide in their comrades. Instead, soldiers who had finished their tour of duty were flown home to arrive "back in the world" often within days, and sometimes hours, of their last combat with the enemy. There were no fellow soldiers to meet them and to serve as a sympathetic sounding board for their experiences; no one to convince them of their own sanity. Nor were there parades or civic tributes.

The presence of a Vietnam veteran in uniform in his hometown was often the occasion for glares and slurs. He was not told that he had fought well; nor was he reassured that he had done only what his country and fellow citizens had asked him to do. Instead of reassurance there was often condemnation—baby killer, murderer—until he too began to question what he had done and, ultimately, his sanity. The result was that at least 500,000—perhaps as many as 1,500,000—returning Vietnam veterans suffered some degree of psychiatric debilitation, called Post-Traumatic Stress Disorder, an illness which has become associated in the public mind with an entire generation of soldiers sent to war in Vietnam.

In the next major conventional war, there will be no need to await one's homecoming to question one's actions or emotions. The nature of modern war will force the confrontation with one's self right on the field of fire. And in most cases the outcome will be psychiatric collapse. Past wars were often horrible enough. Modern war has become so intense, lethal, and destructive that most normally sane men can no longer endure it. The soldier's mind just won't bear the burden, and most will be driven mad.

But must we remain trapped in a practice that can no longer realistically succeed? If major conventional wars can no longer achieve national political goals and if soldiers can no longer fight them without most being driven insane, must we persist in fighting them anyway? There are some who suggest that war is part of man's genetic aggressive inheritance. In this view war cannot be banished. For others, war is a perversion of man's natural instincts, a function of environment or social interaction. Such people think that the scourge of war can be eliminated by reason and education. Both perspectives, I believe, are wrong.

If it is true that man is, by nature, an aggressive predator, it remains an open question whether or not natural drives toward aggression need necessarily be expressed in full-scale war. It may not be possible to banish war but it is possible to banish certain types of wars. The forms of man's aggression are learned and seem related to two variables: the nature of social organization and the state of technology. Each or both can be changed.

In primitive societies the conduct of war was limited by the relative simplicity of their social and organizational structures. Most tribes could not support a special caste of warriors whose full-time job was war. Rather, wars were fought by hunters who were pressed into military service when they were needed. This made it difficult to plan for war and even more difficult to dedicate the society's resources to war in advance of an actual conflict. As societies grew larger and more complex they became marked by the emergence of special groups who performed specific functions—gatherers, hunters, farmers, traders, priests. It was only then that it became possible to develop a professional warrior caste whose sole task was to prepare for and fight wars.

Once a military caste came into being, it could lay claim to a share of the society's resources on the grounds that they were needed to protect the society in the event of war. Until the twentieth century, the influence of warrior castes on societies—with the few notable exceptions of warrior societies such as the Mongols in the twelfth century—was routinely less than that of other castes. In our century the advent of total war required that all elements of a society be integrated into the military effort. This requirement moved the military castes to the forefront in terms of their ability to influence society and to command its resources.

A second variable that profoundly affects the nature of war is technology. Once states began to develop a high degree of social differentiation, the size and specialization of the military task called into existence specific industries to provide the military with weapons and matériel. The result was the emergence of a permanent armaments industry. As time passed, military organization itself increasingly generated pressures for the development of new armaments, until the task of weapons development, heretofore largely confined to the civilian sector, was turned over almost completely to the military. The warriors were responsible for developing their own tools of the trade. The most defining characteristic of a modern nation-state is its ability to maintain large standing armies and large quantities of sophisticated weapons.

Modern societies have marshaled the total resources of the state for purposes of war. We have developed weapons technologies whose power to destroy has reached almost unthinkable levels. We cannot "disinvent" our social institutions. But that is not the real question. The real issue is whether man can find a way to fight wars without necessarily raising the level of hostilities to the point of self-destruction. The fact that social institutions and military technologies exist in no way automatically compels their use for total war. There remains a very real choice.

The decision to employ a weapons technology depends rationally upon an assessment that it will convey advantages that the enemy does not have. But in conventional war, such advantages are seldom evident and often illusory. Both sides usually possess very similar weapons and therefore their use will not convey any significant military advantage. The only result of their employment will be to escalate the slaughter with neither side gaining any advantage. If plans are formulated on the assumption that certain weapons will be used, then they almost certainly will be used. But again, there is nothing inevitable about this. It would be just as wise, and somewhat more realistic, to plan to fight wars at lower levels of intensity since high-intensity wars promise only greater and greater levels of death with no accompanying military advantage. Infatuation with military technology, when it ignores the fact that the enemy has the same technology, becomes nothing short of suicidal.

The use of weapons produced by the most sophisticated technology makes no sense when it threatens to destroy the society's human and moral fabric. In these circumstances, the use of military technology becomes a sterile exercise in technique. War is no longer the means to larger ends, but becomes an end in itself. There are many historical examples of nations that chose to forgo the use of certain technologies because they threatened the existence of values that were central to their society. For example, the Greek city-states persistently refused to adopt more lethal Persian military technology on the grounds that it was indiscriminate in its killing power and threatened the social and moral values upon which the Greek warrior ethos was built. They sustained this refusal for almost four hundred years.

Japanese society in the sixteenth century, after being introduced to firearms by the Portuguese, quickly produced the best marksmen and firearms in all of Asia. Previously the samurai had limited combat to swords and lances and allowed no one but trained warriors to engage in war, and the impact of the rifle on this feudal military order was disastrous. Within a few decades, the Japanese warlords were using rifles and, worse, had begun to organize mass armies through conscription of heretofore noncombatants. Equipping the peasantry with long-range rifles had the predictable effect of greatly increasing the level of violence and lethality, which in turn threatened to destroy the fabric of Japanese life. Seeing that the new technology no longer conferred any military advantages and threatened to destroy the nature of the society, the Japanese warlords agreed to outlaw firearms. Weapons were confiscated and destroyed and the manufacture of new weapons was punishable by death. By the time the Americans "opened up" Japan three hundred years later, the Japanese had completely lost the knowledge of how to make firearms.

During the Middle Ages the use of certain weapons, most notably the morning star, was restricted to designated combatants. The invention of gunpowder, which, in the West, did more to increase the destructiveness of weaponry than any other invention except the splitting of the atom, was regarded by its Chinese inventors as merely a curiosity. The Chinese were well aware of the potential of gunpowder, but refused to use it for weapons on the grounds that Chinese society and its military forces were already so morally superior as to require no further inventions at all. The infamous "gut runner" bayonet invented by the Swiss in the seventeenth century was rejected by all "civilized" armies of the time. The experience with poison gas in World War I led to the refusal of even the Nazi regime to use it in World War II even though it faced certain defeat without it. The Geneva Convention of 1923 represents a systematic effort by the nations of the world to proscribe the use of certain weapons and to establish more humane rules of war. In the nuclear era, most nations of the world are signatories to the nuclear nonproliferation pact designed to prevent the spread of nuclear weapons. The superpowers have come to a number of agreements designed to proscribe the development of certain weapons. The agreement in 1963 to ban atmospheric testing has lasted for twenty-three years and has prohibited the development of a number of refinements of nuclear weapons. After the 1971 treaty dealing with chemical weapons the United States destroyed almost its complete stock of chemical weapons and the Soviets agreed to limit their stockpiles and produce no more. The treaty between the U.S.S.R. and the United States in 1975 successfully stopped the development of anti-ballistic missiles and prevented the militarization of space. This agreement has also prohibited the deployment of anti-satellite weapons. The SALT I and SALT II agreements have actually reduced the number of launchers and warheads that both sides maintain and for ten years prevented the development of new strategic missiles. What these agreements show is that it is possible for men in modern times to limit the technology of war just as the ancients did. To be sure, because of their size and complexity, it is more difficult for modern states to achieve such agreements. Nonetheless the task is not insurmountable.

There are, then, a number of historical precedents for restricting the use and development of military technology. There is even more precedent in history for using existing technologies in a manner designed to preserve the social functions of war while limiting casualties. Ceremonial war has long sociological roots going back to the individual combats between warriors to decide the fate of peoples. The battle between David and Goliath is such an example. And Greek literature is rife with stories about individuals who chose to fight as champions of their city-states. The medieval jousting matches between warrior knights are part of the same tradition. In more modern times, American Indian warriors, until corrupted by the more advanced weaponry introduced by the white man, regarded killing a man in battle as dishonorable. Instead of killing another warrior, no difficult task if he was taken from ambush, the mark of a truly brave warrior was to creep up on his foe and touch him with a stick—counting coup—and then run away. Getting close enough to touch an enemy was sufficient proof that he could be killed. Killing him was superfluous and not an occasion of honor. In New Guinea, prior to World War II, native tribes would often engage in warfare. But since people and resources were scarce, they minimized the carnage. New Guinea warriors were excellent shots with a bow and arrow. But when war broke out, warriors on all sides would remove the feathers from their arrows. It was the feathers which gave the arrow stability in flight and thus increased its accuracy. Without them, the arrows could hardly hit anything. It was with such arrows that tribes fought each other. Moreover, all sides had any number of other lethal weapons—clubs, spears, lances. Generally, however, the tribes chose not to use them precisely because they were so lethal.

The history of military technology demonstrates that it is not impossible to sustain the social institution of war while limiting its effects by restricting the use of weapons that are so destructive that they threaten to destroy the social fabric. This allows a society to maintain the social institution of war along with the status and excitement it conveys to the warriors but without destroying the society itself. In the past the values of a society or the warrior's code limited the carnage of war. What is needed to secure the future is for men to restore the balance between means and ends, the balance between values and technology. If not, then technology will control our values—as it has begun to do since World War II—and technology will become the only end for which a society exists.

Some critics would argue that even if it were possible to limit the number and types of weapons it would still be impossible to "disinvent" them. By this they mean that the knowledge of how to manufacture sophisticated weapons would remain. To some extent this is true. However, the fact is that technologies of all sorts are routinely disinvented. After the fall of Rome almost the entire spectrum of Roman military technology—ballistas, crossbows, siege machinery, military mapping—disappeared from the inventory of warfare for more than a thousand years. Most of it was not reinvented again until the Renaissance. The Japanese certainly lost their knowledge of gunpowder and rifle manufacturing until it was regained from the Americans in the 1840s. More recently, the ability of the U.S. military to build the KH-11 spy satellite, the mainstay of the American spy satellite program until 1982, was lost. Manufacture of the KH-11 was discontinued after it was replaced by the KH-14. The KH-14, a larger and heavier satellite, was designed to be launched by the space shuttle. When the shuttle exploded in 1986, there were no vehicles capable of launching the KH-14. The Department of Defense discovered to its horror that the design teams and parts manufacturers needed to produce the KH-11 were no longer in existence.

The fact is that modern weapons systems are so complex that they require special teams to manufacture and assemble them. Much of the technology is "thin"—that is, highly dependent on small numbers of specially trained men. Once such teams are dispersed, the functional ability to produce a weapons system is lost and cannot easily be reestablished. Most weapons technology of the past was "thick," in that it could be built and maintained by almost anyone with modest skill. Moreover, if a production and design team is disassembled, the actual knowledge of how a system is produced disappears. People forget how the system worked and how it was assembled. The analogy might be drawn with modern personal computers. There are upward of thirty million personal computers in the United States. Few of those who use them understand their technical workings or can repair them if need be. There are fewer than 100,000 computer repairmen in the country. If, by some accident, all of them were to disappear, within weeks computer technology would cease to function. Within a year the knowledge of how to fix them would also disappear. If it were indeed possible to solve the psychological basis of war, the problem of actually "disinventing" the knowledge of weapons technology would present only minor difficulties.

The problem of limiting the carnage of war is fundamentally psychological. As Carl Sagan has said, the problem is to change the way we think. Men do not fear because they possess weapons, they build weapons because they fear. The same nuclear weapons which in the Soviet arsenal provoke fear in Americans are readily accepted when they are in the possession of the British or the French. British and French nuclear arsenals are each capable of inflicting well over thirty million casualties in an attack on the United States. Yet there is no fear. Indeed, weapons that once provoked fear because they were in the hands of the Chinese (Dean Rusk's great fear of the "yellow peril" during the Vietnam War) no longer do so since America's rapprochement with the Chinese in 1971. None of this means that war can be eliminated but only that it is possible for the psychological basis of war, fear, to be altered. And if the psychological basis of war can be changed, then it is possible to limit the carnage of war either by limiting the development of certain weapons or by limiting their use.

The shocking truth is that the military establishments of the modern state can no longer provide security and protection. Rather, the continued development of weaponry can only increase the probability that societies will eventually be destroyed. Each side sustains an enormous military establishment which siphons off ever-increasing social resources under the guise of defense while, in truth, each military caste can only offer the prospect of greater and greater destruction that, in the name of defense, will be visited upon their respective societies. We long ago reached this point in the development of nuclear weapons and we have now reached the same point with conventional weapons.

In the modern nation-state the cultural values of the society no longer govern the pace and direction of the military establishment. The reverse is true. An ever more complex social organization increases the mystery of sophisticated military technology while at the same time fragmenting social relationships, subgroups, and values which used to provide the basis for the average man to make judgments about civic issues. The extraordinary complexity of modern military weapons and their place in the overall strategic picture put them beyond the understanding of the ordinary citizen. The individual no longer feels capable of judging and he willingly transfers the responsibility to others, notably the generals and the politicians. Unfortunately, these actors have a vested interest in perpetuating the game and so it goes on. One of the tragedies of modern war is that whole societies may be exterminated and their citizens will never know why.

If there are examples in history of cultures which restricted forms of social organization and military technology in order to place limits on war, there is also a clear record of cultures which refused to do so. Without exception, each of these states, after a period of expansion, conquest, and dominance, was destroyed by war. The empires of the Egyptians, Darius, Alexander, Caesar, Genghis Khan, Napoleon, and Hitler were all destroyed in turn by more powerful military forces. If there is any one lesson in history it is that war does not guarantee the survival of nation-states. It is far more likely to destroy the societies which wage them. If this has been true throughout history, it is no less certain today, when the staggering levels of military power can no longer guarantee anything but mutual suicide.

There is nothing inevitable about using military technologies or even using them in certain ways. Even if man is innately aggressive, how he expresses this aggression is very much, as it has always been, the consequence of the human ability to choose. While military technology appears to have a life of its own, there is nothing inevitable in this fact. Human choice and will can, as in the past, reverse the trend and stop the momentum. The requirement is that we learn to change how we think about war. To believe that war is inevitable, that existing technologies must be used, is truly a counsel of despair. Indeed, it is a counsel of certain death.

Yet the game goes on despite all the evidence that sane and normal men can no longer stand the stress of battle in modern war, despite the evidence that only the truly insane will survive the horror on the battlefields of the future. Americans have, for the most part, been exempt from the genuine tragedy of war and, as a consequence, seem more ready to accept their myths about war. They have never endured the reality against which other nations readily measure the cost of combat. And this makes us a very dangerous people.

While almost all sane men are subject to breakdown under fire, this does not preclude the possibility that soldiers of one culture may be subject to more rapid mental collapse than others. The American culture seems to have within it strains which make the susceptibility of its soldiers to psychiatric breakdown greater than for, say, Russian or Chinese soldiers. Certainly the American Army in World War II suffered more psychiatric casualties than any other army involved in that war. The Japanese Army had almost no psychiatric casualties at all. German and Russian rates were about the same, nine men per thousand, while the British rates were somewhat higher but still below those of the United States.

By any standard, life in the United States is comfortable. Most Americans are strangers to heavy physical labor. Few are ever cold or hungry, and even fewer are threatened by harsh governmental action, which, if nothing else, breeds a sense of perseverance and discipline in the face of events over which one has no control. If Americans believe anything, it is that they have control over their own destinies and that human intervention can overcome almost any obstacle.

Such an outlook will make it difficult for Americans to endure over long periods under conditions which are beyond their control. Foreign observers have long noted that an inability to wait patiently for changes over the long run is a major characteristic of American foreign and economic policy. Americans are addicted to the quick fix, rooted strongly in their belief that no set of circumstances can persist for very long in the face of human initiative and careful planning. This attitude is supported by the American belief in the wonders of science and technology. Indeed, historically Americans have tended to use machines to deal with difficult human problems. When it was clear in the 1970s that the American Army was attracting only volunteers who had lower than average intelligence, rather than face the politically unpopular choice of returning to a draft to get a more representative cross section of American youth, the military embarked upon a program to make weapons simpler to use. This solution made it possible to avoid the wider social problem of drafting the more well-to-do and politically powerful classes. Americans have always seen technology as the solution to human problems and continue to do so today. No clearer example could be offered than the determination of the American military to turn to science to develop a chemical fix to deal with the problem of psychiatric collapse in battle.

Besides a lack of social discipline and the romance with

technology, American society creates additional barriers to producing a soldier used to and able to endure hardship. American society is less like other societies in that it is comprised of a number of less tightly knit subgroups in which the individual finds succor and reassurance. American society is highly fragmented. Americans are more apt than most people to pride themselves on being individuals with few attachments to others which are not based on mutual utility. The society, after all, is based on the premise that the highest social good results from the pursuit of individual self-interest with few concerns about the common good levied upon individual behavior. The ideological bedrock of American society rests on the premises of Smithian economics, Madisonian politics, Darwinian social ethics, and psychological egoism, all of which assert that somehow millions of individuals pursuing their own economic, political, social, and personal interests equates, by some invisible guiding hand, to the common good. Thus, Americans tend to build fewer and much weaker ties to groups than Soviet or Israeli citizens do.

This reduction of much of society to individualists instead of groups is reflected in and simultaneously maintained by a number of social factors. The extended family, so common in other countries, is almost nonexistent in the United States. It has been destroyed by a high rate of social and geographical mobility. It is remarkable that over thirty million Americans move every year. To be sure, many move only a few miles away from "home," but just as many move out of state or to another section of the country. Ties to the extended family barely exist, severed as they are by geographical dispersion. Nor is the nuclear family, the primary generator of social attachments and group values, faring much better. The divorce rate in the country is approaching 50 percent and for some age groups, those in their thirties, promises to reach 60 percent. More and more households are comprised of single-parent "families," and more and more are headed by women who are vulnerable to a range of social forces that make it difficult to encourage their children to establish strong ties to anything or anyone. Whole generations of children have been raised with few strong attachments to others and have learned time and again the lesson that commitments to others can lead to betrayal and disappointment. In such circumstances it is not surprising that we are becoming a nation of isolated individuals with little in the way of group cohesion.

For some the isolation is intolerable. We are, as Aristotle wrote, social animals and probably bond to one another for the same reasons that herd animals do. But America's social structure presents formidable obstacles to social bonding and often exacts high economic and social costs for those who do bond. Isolation often fosters despair, and despair leads to other pathologies. Consider, for example, that the American rate of suicide among its youth is the highest in the world and that is counting only the obvious suicides. There is a good case to be made that many of the deaths on the nation's highways, particularly those in single-car accidents, are really suicides. Unable to endure the isolation or the pathologies isolation has induced, many Americans simply self-destruct.

Moreover, the lack of social moorings has led Americans to become an addictive society. No country in the world, for example, is more susceptible to faddish behavior. Sociologists have known for years that participating in a fad—new clothes, music, cars, food—is really an attempt by social isolates to establish a sense of being part of a larger group that can define itself as special. The desire to participate in a fad is really the desire to ward off the isolation that much of American life often imposes. Clever advertising exploits the desire to make friends, to be popular, to be chic, and to be accepted. The longing to belong is also found in the very high rate of American drug addiction.

The extent of drug addiction in the United States is appalling. In 1985 42 percent of all Americans smoked marijuana at least once; 30 percent of all college students had

tried cocaine; 12 percent of all college students had tried
hallucinogens; 38 percent of all youth had tried some drug
stronger than marijuana before reaching their twenty-fifth
birthday.[1] In addition, one in every six high school students
will have tried cocaine before his or her senior year and 40
percent of college graduates will have tried it. More than 17
percent of college students used cocaine more than once
before they graduated.[2] Heroin, no longer the drug of choice,
still has 500,000 daily users, and cocaine claims five million
addicts, many of them members of the nation's most pros-
perous classes.[3] In the workplace, drug addiction has become a national menace. One estimate is that 21 percent of
the industrial work force uses cocaine, a fact which costs
industry twenty-five billion dollars a year in lost production.[4] None of this includes the addiction to alcohol, which
is by far the most serious addiction of the American people.
It is estimated that two-thirds of all auto fatalities, about
40,000 deaths a year, are caused by drunk drivers.

Finally, isolation is readily reflected in the nation's addiction to unreality. Television is the national addiction. The
average American spends almost one-third of his waking
hours—almost seven and a half hours a day—in front of the
television set. Competing sources of information have diminished almost to the vanishing point. What appears on
the television screen becomes reality. Television news becomes virtually the only source of information. What is particularly troubling is the degree to which Americans tend to
attribute reality to television shows. Many Americans are
addicted to soap operas and strongly identify with specific
characters as if they were involved in real situations. One
has only to watch or listen to the emotional reactions of
audiences to television sitcoms to appreciate the depth of
attachment that many have to TV personalities. For many,
television and movie characters become role models, an understandable reaction to social situations which, in their own
lives, are fragmented.

All of this tends to make American society a fragile one and leaves its members unaccustomed to dealing with even everyday stress. American psychiatrists estimate that as many as one-third of all Americans on any given day are psychologically debilitated to a degree great enough to impair their ability to function normally at work and in their social relationships![5] These same estimates suggest that at least this many may be debilitated enough to require professional help. The incidence of "abnormal behavior patterns" in American society is dangerously high. In 1981, the last year for which complete data are available, there were 27,300 suicides, 1,200,000 people suffering from "active" schizophrenia, 16,000,000 suffering from anxiety or phobia, 18,000,000 suffering from major depression and other affective disorders (300,000 of which were hospitalized for depression), 13,000,000 alcoholics (including 3,000,000 teenagers), 10,200,000 people arrested for serious crimes, 29,000 schoolchildren suffering from some sort of psychosis, 3,500,000 elementary school children suffering moderate to severe emotional problems, and 34,000,000 people affected by some mental disorder.[6]

In addition to major problems with addictive drugs, the society is also rife with chemical solutions to human problems—diet pills, tranquilizers, stimulants, uppers, downers, pills for heartburn, constipation, upset stomach, headaches, pills to put one to sleep and pills to wake one up. All these "chemical solutions" are touted as quick fixes to the human ailments of stress, self-image, and lack of confidence.

Just what kind of soldiers can such a society produce? Surely, the new recruit from which the soldier must be fashioned has a range of difficulties and problems, especially a lack of discipline and endurance to stress, that are not shared by the soldiers of other nations who are brought up in more stable social and group relationships. It may be that we are not a people well equipped for war. Whatever else the American soldier is capable of, he may not be very capable of endurance. There is little in the prior social experience of the American soldier that has taught him to endure.

Confronted with these facts and having to find a solution to the very high rates of psychiatric collapse that will be generated by modern conventional war, it is not at all surprising that the American military establishment has turned to the chemical quick fix. Such technological approaches to solving human problems have been the traditional manner in which we, as a people, have tried to solve difficulties. But if we succeed in developing a chemical solution for psychiatric collapse—as it seems sure we will in the next five years or so—the human costs will be immense and will certainly outweigh whatever gains in military power that can reasonably be expected.

Apart from genuine moral repugnance at the transformation of the citizen soldier into a true sociopath so that he can fulfill his military duty, there is the question of basic rights. Does the obligation of a citizen to defend his country extend to the point where he must quite literally surrender his sanity? Does it make any moral sense to require the soldier to transform his very nature in order to meet his obligation? What military goals could possibly justify such a trade-off? No doubt some will argue that only by administering a chemical preventive for stress is it possible for the soldier to have any real chance of survival in modern war. While this may be an accurate restatement of the problem, it does little to answer the larger question of whether or not the price of physical survival is legitimately purchased at the cost of mental destruction. If soldiers on all sides must be made chemically similar in order to fight, how are the values of the societies which send them into battle to be meaningfully distinguished? And even if they could be distinguished, such distinctions will be meaningless to the soldiers, who, as a result of chemically induced sociopathy, will be unable to make sense in any case of emotional attachments to values.

To be sure, the soldier will probably be given the choice of whether to take a stress-preventive drug, but the choice will not be real. With the alternatives of being driven mad by fear or reducing that fear by the simple expedient of a daily pill, both unit peer pressure (how can one depend upon a man who may collapse under pressure when the rest of the men in the unit do not feel similar fear?) and the evidence of his own senses when exposed to the horror of the modern battlefield will combine to make genuine choice an illusion. Even if the soldier initially resists taking an anxiety-preventive drug, a day or two in battle—if he survives—will be enough to show him the error of his ways.

Nor is there any way of knowing at this stage of the research whether such a drug would have long-term psychiatric effects. It is a fair guess that the chemical compound will remain in the soldier's system for periods of at least weeks after prolonged use. But there is no way to determine to what degree or how long hundreds of thousands of soldiers will be affected by sustained use of the drug. The prospect of having to discharge thousands of emotionally deficient men back into the civilian society after a war is too real—and too frightening—to ignore.

Given the American concern about stress and a little free enterprise, it would not be long before such a chemical preventive found its way—legally or illegally—into the civilian population. After all, there are any number of occupations in civilian life that induce high levels of stress. The temptation to prevent the onset of stress on a day-to-day basis would be almost irresistible. Worse, judging from the staggering amount of stress-controlling drugs that are already consumed by the general public—drugs such as Librium, Valium, alcohol, in addition to cocaine and heroin—there is no reason to suspect that a chemical which permits or even enhances normal mental awareness and function would not soon become the "drug of choice" for millions. The prospect of a largely sociopathic society then becomes frighteningly real.

What has happened, of course, is that man has evolved to a point where his implements of war, even conventional war, have become so lethal that his mind can no longer endure the fighting. He has reached a point where either he must become insane if he wishes to fight or he must find other ways of settling conflicts. It remains an open question whether the physical destruction of millions of human beings is, in fact, not preferable to their continued survival if the price of that survival may change the very nature of the human mind—and soul—as we have known it. A society of sociopaths devoid of emotional feeling may simply be too high a cost for men to pay for their own survival. Certainly it might appear so to those who refuse to participate in the chemical fix.

So man must choose. Either he will recognize that the cost of war will be his own humanity or he will find other ways to deal with conflicts between nation-states. History suggests that it is not impossible to "disinvent" certain technologies deemed too destructive of social values; nor is there anything inevitable or irrevocable about the specific forms of social organization that make war likely. Both are creations of man's intellect and will and can be changed by men determined to survive and retain their sanity. Men can and must change the way they think about war. The danger is that they will not see the peril and will proceed on the present course to be destroyed by the enemy or, as seems more likely now, by their own hand. In the effort to escape fear, men in battle have traditionally sought refuge in insanity. For the modern chemical soldier, there is no refuge anymore except an end to war.

Notes

Chapter 1

1. John Keegan, "The Spectre of Conventional War," *Harper's Magazine*, July 1983, p. 10.

2. All facts, figures, and statistics concerning performance characteristics of the weapons discussed in this chapter are taken from official military manuals or performance data published by the manufacturers of the weapons. Two good sources for this information are: FM 100-5, "Operations," U.S. Army publication, 1978, and Tom Gervasi, *America's War Machine* (New York: Grove Press, 1984), which provides an encyclopedic compendium of manufacturers' performance data.

Chapter 2

1. Lawrence Ingraham and Frederick Manning, "Psychiatric Battle Casualties: The Missing Column in the War Without Replacements," *Military Review*, August 1980, p. 21. The same argument is made at length by the same authors in "American Military Psychiatry," in Richard A. Gabriel, *Military Psychiatry: A Comparative Perspective* (Westport, Conn.: Greenwood Press, 1986), Chapter 2.

2. Xenophon, *Anabasis*, Book III, Chapter 1.

3. Gwynne Dyer, *War* (New York: Crown Publishers, 1985), p. 22.

4. Max Hastings, *Military Anecdotes* (New York: Oxford University Press, 1985), p. 18.

5. Ibid., pp. 20–21.

6. Ibid., p. 38.

7. Peter Connolly, *Greece and Rome at War* (Englewood Cliffs, N.J.: Prentice-Hall, 1981), pp. 139–40.

8. Hastings, op. cit., p. 64.

9. Dyer, op. cit., p. 142.

10. Hastings, op. cit., p. 75.

11. Ibid.

12. Ibid., p. 98.

13. Ibid., p. 123.

14. Farley Mowatt, *And No Birds Sang* (Toronto: Bantam, 1979), p. 154.

15. Hastings, op. cit., p. 144.

16. Reuven Gal and Richard A. Gabriel, "Battlefield Heroism in the Israeli Defense Force," *International Social Science Review*, Autumn 1982, pp. 232–35.

17. Hastings, op. cit., p. 145.

18. Richard A. Gabriel and Paul Savage, *Crisis in Command* (New York: Hill and Wang, 1978), p. 182 (Table 3).

19. Hastings, op. cit., pp. 151–52.

20. Ibid.

21. George Rosen, "Nostalgia: A Forgotten Psychological Disorder," *Psychological Medicine*, Vol. 5 (1975), pp. 340–41.

22. Ibid., p. 342.

23. Albert Deutsche, "Military Psychiatry in the Civil War," in *One Hundred Years of American Psychiatry* (New York: Columbia University Press, 1944), p. 377.

24. Franklin Jones, "Future Directions of Military Psychiatry," in Gabriel, *Military Psychiatry*, Chapter 6.

25. Hastings, op. cit., p. 198.

26. Ibid.

27. Ibid., p. 220.

28. Richard A. Gabriel, *The Mind of the Soviet Fighting Man* (Westport, Conn.: Greenwood Press, 1984), pp. 43–44.

29. Evan S. Connell, *Custer: Son of the Morning Star* (New York: Harper & Row, 1984), p. 155.

30. Ibid., p. 313.

31. Ibid., p. 419.

32. Deutsche, op. cit., pp. 370–72.

33. Ibid., p. 377.

34. Ibid., p. 372.

35. Richard A. Gabriel, *Soviet Military Psychiatry* (Westport, Conn.: Greenwood Press, 1986), Chapter 4.

36. Connell, op. cit., pp. 9–12.

37. Ibid., p. 30.

38. Ibid., p. 419.

39. Ibid., p. 55.

40. Ibid., p. 61.

41. Ibid.

42. Ibid., pp. 149–50.

43. Ibid., p. 173.

Chapter 3

1. Sometimes censorship of the horror of war reaches ridiculous proportions. General Douglas Haig, the Supreme Commander of British Forces in World War I, forbade his staff officers to visit the front line. He believed that if they witnessed the horror personally it would affect their ability to plan future military operations objectively.

2. Lawrence Ingraham and Frederick Manning, "American Military Psychiatry," in Richard A. Gabriel, *Military Psychiatry: A Comparative Perspective* (Westport, Conn.: Greenwood Press, 1986), p. 67.

3. Richard A. Gabriel, *Soviet Military Psychiatry* (Westport, Conn.: Greenwood Press, 1986), p. 123.

4. Ingraham and Manning, op. cit., pp. 67–68.

5. *Historical Statistics of the United States* (Washington, D.C.: U.S. Department of Commerce, 1976), p. 1140.

6. Edward A. Strecker, "Military Psychiatry in World War I," in *One Hundred Years of American Psychiatry* (New York: Columbia University Press, 1944), p. 403.

7. This figure is derived by subtracting the number of psychiatric casualties recorded as permanently lost from the number of total psychiatric casualties admitted for treatment at military medical facilities.

8. Eli Ginsberg, *The Lost Divisions* (New York: Columbia University Press, 1950), pp. 91–92.

9. This figure is arrived at by subtracting the total number of psychiatric casualties lost from the total number of admissions to military medical facilities for psychiatric reasons.

10. Gwynne Dyer, *War* (New York: Crown Publishers, 1985), p. 118.

11. Ibid.

12. Ibid.

13. Stewart L. Baker, Jr., "Traumatic War Disorders" (no further source given), p. 1831.

14. *Historical Statistics of the United States*, p. 1140.

15. Ingraham and Manning, op. cit., p. 88.

16. Ibid., p. 91.

17. Gregory Belenky, *Israeli Battle Shock Casualties: 1973 and 1982* (Washington, D.C.: Walter Reed Army Institute of Research Report, 1983), p. 26.

18. David Marlowe, *Cohesion, Anticipated Breakdown, and Endurance in Battle* (Washington, D.C.: Walter Reed Army Institute of Research, 1979), p. 3.

19. Reuven Gal and Richard A. Gabriel, "Battlefield Heroism in the

Israeli Defense Force," *International Social Science Review*, Autumn 1982, pp. 332–35.

20. Lawrence Ingraham and Frederick Manning, "Psychiatric Battle Casualties: The Missing Column in the War Without Replacements," *Military Review*, August 1980, p. 24.

21. Roy L. Swank and Walter E. Marchand, "Combat Neuroses: The Development of Combat Exhaustion," *Archives of Neurology and Psychiatry*, Vol. 55 (1946), p. 244.

22. Jules Masserman, *Principles of Dynamic Psychiatry* (Philadelphia: W. B. Saunders Company, 1961), pp. 180–82.

23. Emanuel Miller, *Neuroses in War* (New York: The Macmillan Company, 1942), p. 87.

24. S. L. A. Marshall, as quoted in Marlowe, op. cit., p. 31.

25. Swank and Marchand, op. cit., p. 238.

26. Ibid.

27. Ibid., p. 240.

28. Ibid., pp. 240–41.

29. Ginsberg, op. cit., p. 91.

30. Swank and Marchand, op. cit., p. 237.

31. Ibid.

32. Miller, op. cit., p. 17.

33. Ibid., p. 229.

34. Ibid., p. 17.

35. Ibid.

36. Ibid., p. 229.

37. Ibid.

38. Ibid., p. 232.

39. Ibid., p. 18.

40. Ibid., p. 230.

Chapter 4

1. Albert Deutsche, "Military Psychiatry in the Civil War," in *One Hundred Years of American Psychiatry* (New York: Columbia University Press, 1944), p. 377.

2. Richard A. Gabriel, *Soviet Military Psychiatry* (Westport, Conn.: Greenwood Press, 1986), pp. 35–36.

3. Ibid.

4. Edward A. Strecker, "Military Psychiatry in World War I," in *One Hundred Years of American Psychiatry*, p. 386.

5. Lawrence Ingraham and Frederick Manning, "American Military Psychiatry," in Richard A. Gabriel, *Military Psychiatry: A Comparative Perspective* (Westport, Conn.: Greenwood Press, 1986), p. 61.

6. Strecker, op. cit., p. 388.

7. Ingraham and Manning, op. cit., pp. 61–63.

8. Ibid., p. 67.

9. Ibid.

10. Ibid., p. 75.

11. Lawrence Ingraham and Frederick Manning, "Psychiatric Battle Casualties: The Missing Column in the War Without Replacements," *Military Review*, August 1980, p. 24.

12. Roy L. Swank and Walter E. Marchand, "Combat Neuroses: The Development of Combat Exhaustion," *Archives of Neurology and Psychiatry*, Vol. 55 (1946), p. 244.

Chapter 5

1. This statement is attributed to a widely respected U.S. Army colonel, Harry Summers of the U.S. Army War College faculty.

2. Richard A. Gabriel, *Soviet Military Psychiatry* (Westport, Conn.: Greenwood Press, 1986), p. 114.

3. The information about the Koyak and Wiros tribes was presented in a lecture by Dr. Lowell Roberts of the Department of Psychology, Rutgers University, at St. Anselm College on October 18, 1985. The paper has not been published yet.

4. Interview with Richard Hechtl, chairman of the Department of Psychology, St. Anselm College. Hechtl is a widely respected expert in the area of sociopathic behavior.

Chapter 6

1. Boston *Globe*, July 16, 1986, p. 15.

2. NBC news report, July 6, 1986.

3. *Newsweek*, June 16, 1986, p. 15.

4. Ibid.

5. This estimate was provided by staffers at the National Institute of Mental Health. It is a figure routinely used by psychiatrists at mental health conferences.

6. These figures were assembled from official government statistics and appear in John M. Darley et al., *Psychology* (Englewood Cliffs, N.J.: Prentice-Hall, 1984), p. 503.